At Your *Service*

At Your *Service*

The Life of a Master Inn Holder

Service Is Our Specialty!

John Mawdsley

Library of Congress Control Number: 2013923717
ISBN: Hardcover   978-1-4931-3980-4
                Softcover   978-1-4931-3978-1
                Ebook   978-1-4931-3979-8

This book was printed in the United States of America.

Rev. date: 01/23/2014

To order additional copies of this book, contact:
Xlibris Corporation
0-800-644-6988
www.xlibrispublishing.co.uk
Orders@xlibrispublishing.co.uk
521739

Contents

*Although this book is largely based on true events in my life,
I have used some artistic licence and fictionalised some dialogue,
characters and occurrences for entertainment purposes.*

Acknowledgements

First and foremost Gaby, who's sheer love and dedication in giving me the strength to combat all the difficulties thrown at me and driving 500 miles each week and to the friends who helped with driving Gaby to ease the burden.

Thanks to the medical team at Southport hospital i.e. Dr Salmi and Sue Perri Davies. The Master Innholders and my colleagues in the industry in providing my electric wheelchair and the Cheshire Forest Hunt for providing my electronic gadgetry.

My 2 Daughters Angeligue and Christine for all their help to me and their Mother Gaby. To my Brother whose tremendous support with looking after Gaby and visiting me each week, driving 200 miles and contacting Gaby each night to check if She was alright.

Last, but not least Linda Innes, my ghostwriter.

Prologue

Service Is Our Specialty!

There are times when I sit in my conservatory in Cheshire, admiring the rolling countryside which sprawls out invitingly before me, and I imagine that I might go for a ride—forgetting for a few precious moments why I cannot.

I picture myself on my faithful horse—The Gambler—and all I can hear is the sound of my own heart beating wildly to the familiar rhythm of his galloping hooves—reminding me what a joy it is to be alive.

Riding is a great passion of mine, one of many. I have always been drawn to the wildness of it and the simple delight of feeling the wind on my face and the sun on my back.

I think it must have started—this love affair with all things equestrian—with a little wooden horse I had as a child. I used to take that thing with me everywhere—pulling it along noisily on its unsteady wheels. No doubt it appealed to the toddler in me and gave me a heightened sense of my own capabilities. I quite simply wouldn't leave it alone. On that horse, I imagined riding over vast fields and across rivers—I was its master and, in turn, master of myself.

Sadly, life does not always follow the carefully laid plans of our imaginations. If I had known, then, that nearly seventy years later I would fall from a real horse and very nearly not survive to tell the tale, I might have been a little more cautious with my aspirations, but one cannot alter time and I would not have given up those idyllic childhood dreams for anything in the world.

The details of my accident are still somewhat confused in my mind—like fragments of a dream which I need help assembling into some sort of coherent order. It happened eight years ago, and since that day I have been confined to a rather private, immobile world—one which I live largely in my mind.

It was not my first riding accident; I had had several before it, one of which had left me with a rather painful broken pelvis and my wife, Gaby, distraught. Not for the first time, I had abandoned her to cope alone with an injured husband, two children and a demanding business and yet, as always, she managed beautifully.

But this time it was different. I would not get up and dust myself down as I had done so often in the past. This time, I would not get up at all.

Finding myself sitting in a wheelchair, as opposed to the soft, leather seat of a sports car or the saddle of a much-loved horse, has been a bitter pill to swallow. This is, after all, no way for a man of spirit and adventure to live, yet it is my life nonetheless and I owe it to Gaby and to myself to live it to the full, as I always have done.

When I am not feeling quite so tragic, I have to admit that I have had more than my fair share of good fortune too. I have a beautiful wife and two lovely daughters and a lifetime of stories to tell my grandchildren—especially when I see that all-too-familiar sadness creep into their eyes as they question why their grandfather cannot lift them above his head as other grandfathers do.

I tell them of the time I raced the legendary Stirling Moss from a vineyard in Burgundy to the port at Calais—and won. I tell them, too, how I was on good terms with the ravishing screen idol Sophia Loren, and I share with them wonderful, treasured stories of my time working for the Queen Mother; stories which must remain discreet, for us alone to enjoy. But most of all, I tell them what a wonderful life this is—a life worth fighting for, as my father did and his father before him.

Fighting is a part of me, which I think I must have learned many years ago, as a young boy during the war. I was just an ordinary lad back then, but I had a head full of extraordinary dreams. By day, I kicked a ball around with the neighbourhood children and hunted for bugs in our garden, yet in the wonderful world of my imagination I was something quite different—rich and famous and fearless, an intrepid explorer. It is hard to reconcile those very early memories with the ones that followed soon after—when war was declared and the air became heavy with the fearful anticipation of what the future might bring. Then the dreams turned into nightmares and my only real aspiration was to survive this wretched thing which threatened us all.

I put up a brave front for a while, hoping that if I ignored the war, it might also ignore me, but it didn't. The simple truth was that things were changing all around me and I couldn't do a thing about it.

As I look back on my life now, I see that those hardships—those early battles fought and occasionally even won, shaped me into the man I am today and filled me with real courage and strength. I need it now, of course, more than ever—that inner strength which promises to make heroes of us all. And yet, in spite of everything, I remain grateful, for the good things and the not so good—the frightening and the exhilarating. It's been a grand life, so far. So let's begin.

War boy

The mouse kept perfectly still; hoping, no doubt, to go unnoticed. What it failed to realise was that mice, when pitched against determined ten-year-old boys, seldom do go unnoticed.

"Come on John, let's grab it!"

My friend Michael was keen to have the whole business over with, and, being children, we thought nothing of what we were about to do. Silently and skilfully, we trapped the poor creature in an old tin box, like a smaller version of the steel cage I used to clamber into with my parents during air raids. I recalled those claustrophobic nights now, as I looked down at our own little prisoner and thought briefly of letting it go. But I didn't—we were boys, after all, and this was what boys did.

Looking back on it now, with the benefit of age and wisdom, I realise, of course, that catching mice and blowing them up—I'm particularly ashamed of that part—was an appalling and cruel pastime. But then, we had lived through appalling and cruel times.

The year was 1946 and Britain was emerging from the war—morally victorious, yet physically broken. Birmingham—where I had lived most of my life—was facing the very daunting task of rebuilding itself and everywhere you went, there were haunting reminders of those terrifying night-time raids.

It's hard to imagine what it was like today, when wars—even our own—take place on someone else's soil, but back then it was very much a part of our everyday lives. I had grown used to seeing brick and rubble, collapsed buildings and huge craters where the roads and pavements ought to have been. Hitler's pilots must have taken a particular dislike to us, because we were bombed relentlessly and I still remember emerging from our shelter on those cold, quiet mornings and wondering which of the houses on my street would still be standing.

The war had robbed so many of so much. For my part, I had lost my father and the careless innocence of my childhood—both of which I would mourn for many years to come. So I suppose, in light of all this, my own, shameful little pastime didn't seem quite so terrible and besides, it gave me an excuse to play with Michael.

"Ready?"

Michael stood poised with the tin box in one hand and our crude, home-made bomb in the other. He set it down carefully and ran to join me in the bushes. From the safety of our hiding place, we witnessed the gruesome scene with a mixture of pride and horror—all the while reminding ourselves that this was what boys did.

I had met Michael at school—Leighton House, and he and his family lived just up the hill from my grandparents, where I had lived for most of the war. By the time I met Michael, I had already been living with my grandparents for a while, but I had started life with my parents in a very comfortable house in Olton, on the outskirts of the city.

When Michael and I weren't tormenting mice, we played with the various gadgets we had each received for Christmases and birthdays, cycled the uneven paths near our houses together and played war games with my Lancaster Bombers—all the things which form the basis of a true and lasting friendship.

It's funny how a child's mind works—I had been genuinely horrified by the air raids over our city while the war was going on; yet now, protected by the newly-acquired safety of 1946, I thought nothing of playing with those model warplanes—soaring them high above my head and then swooping them down again to land with an exaggerated crash.

My father had made them for me out of aluminium, while he was posted with the RAF, attached to Bomber Command, in North Africa, and I was understandably very attached to them. The meticulous workmanship and loving hand was so typical of him—a caring and assiduous man whose only mistake in life was to do the right thing.

My father, Eric James Mawdsley, was a slim, handsome, tall man, although not quite as tall as my mother, Rosie Bond, who was part Spanish, part Irish and terribly attractive. They made quite a dashing pair.

My father had a good position with the famous Kardomah coffee company, which had branches all over the country, and we lived a fairly comfortable life.

I loved our house, what I remember of it. It was large and friendly and had a good garden for toddling about in, which was all I was really capable of in those days. But the best part about my life then was that I was still so innocent—blissfully unaware of the changes going on all around me and happily uninitiated into the harsh world of combat which was to form an unhappy backdrop to the rest of my childhood.

For the time being, life was pretty good and I spent most of my time playing with my favourite possession—a little wooden horse on wheels. I dragged that thing along with me everywhere I went, like a puppy, making an awful racket and no doubt getting unseemly scuff marks on my mother's newly-polished floors. I would make up little stories on that horse which, in turn, became bigger stories—exciting treks over rocky mountain ranges, daring encounters with Indian braves—it was a great escape from the growing sense of panic and fear which was slowly finding its way into all of our homes.

As I look back on those years now, with the added benefit of other people's knowledge, history books, picture archives and museum exhibits, I am able to place my early memories within their correct, historical context. If I choose, I can now make some sense of it all, but back then, it was all a bit of a jumble. I quickly forgot some things and remembered others in grave detail, but the one thing I was as sure of then as I am now, is this: war is a disease, from which none of us ever fully recover.

1939 came sadly all too quickly for me and, as far as I'm concerned, it was the last year of my childhood as I knew it. I was barely three years old.

My father did what all the fathers in those days did—he worked hard and he worried, about us and about the bombs which he knew would come. Don't forget, he had lived through one war already and knew something of what to expect. My mother, in turn, played her part beautifully—she fed her boys and built her family and, before long, I had a little sister—Veronica—to play with.

Everyone has their own war stories to tell; some tragic, some heart-warming, some—like fishermen's tales of their catch—slightly exaggerated, but each one, without fail, is touched by death in some way, and mine would prove to be no different. Despite my young years, I could already tell that the world we lived in was no longer a safe and pleasant one. Bombs, like firecrackers, began to fall at night and I learnt what it was to be truly afraid. I wasn't really sure what all the noise and dust meant, but I knew it wasn't good and I longed for things to go back to how they were before.

At the start of 1940, my father thought it best that we move to the country; where he hoped we would all be safer, since the raids over Birmingham were frequent and showed no signs of letting up. I was nearly four by then and life ought to have been a joy. I should have been learning to swim and read and ride a bike, but instead, I was packing my things into a little suitcase and preparing myself for a new and uncertain future.

Fortunately, the house we were moving to was quite lovely and I soon forgot my initial concerns. My parents had bought a charming, wood-beamed cottage in a small village just outside

Stratford-upon-Avon, which was very different to our previous city town-house. There, barricaded from the outside world in our solid new home, we began what we hoped would be a solid new life.

People always say that hindsight is such a wonderful thing, but I find it can be achingly spiteful at times. It allows us to see where we went wrong, but provides us with no way of changing things. If my father had known then what the enemy was planning for the night of the 14th of November 1940, he wouldn't have bothered moving us all; but life stops for no-one, and history will not allow itself to be re-written.

I was in bed that night, sleeping the delightful, untroubled sleep of the young when I was woken by a tremendous noise, like fireworks, and the sound of glass shattering. Young boys can be ever so brave in their games, sword-fighting and swashbuckling, but this was no game. It was the single most terrifying moment of my life and one which I would revisit in my nightmares for many years to come.

Our home had been hit by a stray bomb from a raid over Coventry, which I later discovered had destroyed more than 4,000 homes in total and cost over 600 people their lives. The force of the blast had knocked all our windows out, and us with them—we were literally blown out of our home, which now lay in an angry pile of broken bricks and rubble.

"John! Are you alright?" My mother's frantic voice called out through the smoky, night air. "John?"

I tried to answer, but my voice didn't work, either due to the shock, a lungful of smoke, or a combination of the two; so instead, I managed to scramble out of the debris and run to her. I cannot explain the joy of that embrace—an embrace that affirmed we were alive, and for that brief, disjointed moment in time, nothing else mattered.

Later, I would look on that night as the night I nearly died rather than the night I survived; but for now, we were all grateful to have made it out and none of us dared to think what the future might hold for us.

Fortunately, a crisis, especially one as monumental as this, brings people together, and without a moment's hesitation, the landlord of our local pub—the Bull Inn—offered us a place to stay until we could get ourselves sorted.

So there I was, just starting out in life really, and already I had survived one attempt on my life, a move and the loss of something that had meant a great deal to me—my little wooden horse. It must have been buried under the rubble, and I would think of it for a long time afterwards, hoping it had not been as scared as I was.

Most four-year-olds sleep in a cot. I now slept in a pub, surrounded by the smell of hops and stale cigarettes. It was an odd place for a child, but I quite liked it; we felt strangely safe surrounded by this familiar, stale air and I began to believe that things would be alright after all. I didn't know it then—how could I have? But years later, I would have a place of my own where people would come to stay and I would offer them drinks and good food and a bed for the night—or for several, just as that landlord had done for us all those years ago.

I settled down on that first pub night and fell asleep, but my dreams were noisy and unsettling. If this was what growing up was all about, I thought later, then I was in no hurry for it.

Sent away

"What's up, John? You've got a face as long as Livery Street!"

That's one of my carers, and he's right. I am in danger here of falling into a melancholic torpor. Life couldn't have been all that bad, could it?

We were still comparatively well-off and had all escaped Stratford with our lives. That was something to be celebrated, surely! But none of us felt much like celebrating, least of all my father. His plan to keep us safe had failed, and when the dust settled and the shock wore off somewhat, he took us all back home—to Birmingham.

Being bombed out of our home had left us all with a heightened sense of danger, and my father now felt that he had a personal duty to do something to help put an end to this terrible war. Despite being a father and well past the age for conscription, he decided to sign up and join the RAF. He was a fit man of above average intelligence, certainly capable of serving his country. What he failed to realise however, was that, in doing so, he would be letting down the people he loved the most.

My mother, normally a pragmatic, understanding woman, was enraged by his decision. The lilting, Irish brogue in her was drowned out by the Spanish blood. Her angry arguments were hot and fiery and would surprise us all. She simply couldn't understand why he would risk his life unnecessarily and leave her alone, with two young children to raise, when we could have kept our heads down and survived this miserable war together. Times were hard enough without the added trauma of saying goodbye to the man you loved and depended on, not knowing when you would see him again. I can see, now, what a terrible knock that must have been for her, and yet I was still too young to offer any help or consolation.

"He'll be alright, mum," I said, but I knew I had no right to promise something I neither understood nor knew to be true.

I thought of my father a lot, mostly when I was in bed at night, listening out for the air raid sirens and wondering if he could hear them too. Was he sleeping under the same sky? Would he wake to the same sun? I had no idea where he had gone and yet, to me, it might as well have been the other side of the world, because the only thing that really mattered was that he wasn't with us.

It is impossible to comprehend what life was like for a child during the war, unless you have experienced it first-hand. I never went to sleep at night feeling safe and always listened out for the mournful toll of the sirens. We never really knew if they would sound in time. I had grown accustomed to the sight of ruined buildings and burnt-out houses.

At school, my teachers were very good at distracting us all, and for those brief daylight hours, we almost forgot what was going on around us, until sundown when it started all over again.

In many ways, families are like trees—they have strong roots and grow new branches, come rain or shine, in a way that is both necessary and comfortingly predictable. Nothing affirms life quite like producing more of it, so it seemed perfectly normal to me that my mother chose this time to have her third baby—my brother, Richard. He was born shortly before my father left, and although he was a much-loved, much-wanted child, it now meant that my mother would be alone with three, rather than two, young children to look after.

Until now, I had weathered several storms, but I had always had my parents close to hand throughout, to comfort me when comfort was needed, and tell me that everything would be alright. Children look to their parents for reassurance and love, and somehow, things never seem quite so bad with their hand to hold or their shoulder to rest on. Now, I was one parent down, so I naturally became even more dependent on my mother, which was why it was a particularly harsh blow when she told me she would have to send me away. It was not a decision she took lightly—far from it—and I was luckier than most children my age, in that I would be going to live with her mother and father, in the nearby village of Harborne, but I felt desolate and abandoned none-the-less.

Looking back on it now, it made good sense. My grandparents were more than happy to help in any way they could, and besides, they could afford to send me to a private school, which in those difficult times, was a luxury not to be passed up.

Although I was initially distraught at having to leave my mother and siblings, my grandparents made me feel so welcome right from the start that I soon settled in, and besides, I would make two very important friendships there, which I still believe got me through the worst of the war. The first was with a delightful Airedale called Sue, and the other was with my grandmother's Spanish maid, Pilar.

Sue was one of those dogs you come to look upon as a person more than a pet, and when I think of her now, I realise that she was a lot like me in many ways—independent, strong-minded—even stubborn at times—and a good hunter. I loved that dog out of all proportion and often, when we were under attack at night, I would find my way into her kennel and lie there for a while, basking in her calming, protective warmth.

Pilar offered me a very different form of escape, through something I had never realised could bring such joy. Food! The meals she prepared, even the most frugal, were always so full of flavour and passion—and it was through her that I discovered my own talent for cooking. I may not have had my own mother during those early years, but between this wonderful Spanish cook and a dog with a kind heart, I had something very close to it. And then, of course, there were my grandparents.

Of all my many achievements, the one of which I am most proud is that I am in all things a gentleman, and I really have my grandfather to thank for that. He taught me so much about life, and honesty and fairness—that I am sure I would not have become such a successful businessman had it not been for his firm, yet gentle guidance. He was Irish and my grandmother was Spanish, from Valencia. Her father had sent her and her sister to England to learn the language and both had ended up falling in love and never going back. When Lucica met Pat, the dashing young man with big dreams, she knew she had found the person she would spend the rest of her life with. She had chosen well and my grandfather proved to be a good, hard-working man who went on to make an excellent living from his road asphalt company—Limmer & Trinidad—which he ran with his brother.

It is fair to say that by the time I went to stay with them, my grandparents were very well-off. They had a lovely house with a number of bedrooms and a large rear garden which climbed upwards. We had our own vegetable patch and chicken run, so we managed to eat well despite the rations and cut-backs. But the best part was the shelter. I was used to crouching into the steel one inside my parents' house and had always considered it a terrible hardship. But this one was much larger, made of brick, and was outside, which not only made it feel safer somehow, but also far less frightening.

I was in regular contact with my mother in those years, and learnt that my father had been based in England for a while, then Greece, before being sent to North Africa. My mother showed great strength of character in those difficult times—signing up, herself, to become an ambulance driver for the hospital corps and transporting those who had been injured by the bombs, whilst at the same time coping admirably with my brother and sister.

I missed them all terribly and looked forward to our occasional visits. My mother had made friends with a nearby family who had children of about our age, and my brother and sister and I played with them as normal children do, forgetting briefly that we were not really normal children. All of us had seen things normal children should not see—we had learnt what it was to be scared and worst of all, we had learnt how to hate. I already hated the enemy for taking me away from my mother, but it was nothing compared with the rage I would feel when they took my father, too.

In a former life, Eric Mawdsley had managed coffee houses. He had met and married his sweetheart and together, they had walked the streets of Birmingham arm in arm, planning their future together. Yet somehow this gentle, mild-mannered businessman had become a Sergeant in the RAF. How little sense it made! He was killed, along with many others, fighting for Montgomery against Rommell's army. I can't remember who told me the news—I assume it was my mother, but I think I must have blocked it from my mind as we often do with truly painful things.

For a long time afterwards, I would look at the planes he had made me and try to imagine him flying in one of them. It was impossible to conceive how this gentle Englishman had met such a violent fate on foreign soil, and even harder to imagine growing up without him by my side. But I had a new life now in Harborne, and I owed it to him and my mother to make something of it.

I was already quite friendly with some of the local children, but it wasn't until I started at Leighton House that I met Michael and discovered what true friendship was.

Leighton House was a solid, traditional school run by a headmaster whom I would later come to adore. He was in his late 60s by then, as were most of the staff—the young teachers had all gone to war and we felt a little disjointed without them. Instead of a natural hierarchy of age and experience, we were just young and old, muddling through as best we could and discovering much joy and satisfaction in one another's strengths.

I was a popular boy with a keen interest in football and amateur dramatics. I joined the operatic society, where I enjoyed working backstage—I was far more interested in the technical side of it, rather than spending hours learning lines and rehearsing parts. On one occasion, I had been helping with a stage set involving a ladder and some paint when the most mischievous idea entered my head. I rigged the paint pot carefully so that it would perch on the ladder, above the stage in the main hall.

The following morning, at prayers, I pulled a strategically positioned rope and released my missile—right onto my English master's head! There was a roar of approval and whoops of delight which rose up from the assembly hall like cheers at a football ground. I was their hero—the pupil's champion—daring to do what others had no doubt only dreamt of. It was a marvellous moment and I fully intended to bask in it, and surely would have done so, had it not been for my unamused victim who was now making his way towards me, dripping white paint all over the assembly hall floor and clenching his fists in balls of rage. Needless to say, when he did finally catch up with me, I was given the cane, but even when I looked at those angry, red welts on my hand, all I could really see was the pot of paint reaching its target and I couldn't help a sheepish grin. Michael, being lively and bold like me, thought this was tremendous and the prank earned its rightful place in school folklore.

I am still like that now—daring and spirited, and I see no real harm in it. Life is for living and there had been too little of that in my brief and heavy youth. Still, the boys at school had learnt a valuable lesson that day, and I have no doubt that many of them showed their elders a great deal more respect in future, not wishing to suffer the same, painful punishment as I had.

Meanwhile, at home, I was learning some valuable lessons of my own. Pilar was instructing me in the art of cooking and my grandfather was doing his best to teach me that the more fortunate you are in life, the more humble you must be—both of which would shape me into the man I am today, and left me with many, treasured memories.

From boy to man

Some people have a passion for motor bikes, enjoying the freedom of the open road and the heightened sense of speed. Others prefer boats—taking great pleasure in the gentle, lulling motion of the water and the sheer luxury of it. With me, it has always been cars.

I remember Gaby's amusement when I told her I was planning to ship my MGB sports car over to France on the Queen Elizabeth, for our honeymoon. She thought I was mad, but it was worth the effort just to be able to drive it to her parents' house in Brittany—I felt like a movie star that day.

In many ways, falling in love with a car is much like falling in love with a girl—it leaves a lasting impression and you never forget your first one. I can still clearly remember the first time I was truly dazzled by a car's beauty and often think of it now—tracing its rounded wheel-arch with my fingers and remembering the cool elegance of its leather-upholstered seats . . .

I stood on the gravel driveway, oblivious to the light rain which had already dampened my hair and jacket, and stared, wide-eyed at my grandfather's exquisite 1946 Jaguar—the epitome of style and sophistication. Its handsome, noble lines and charming, round headlamps were so perfectly matched, it seemed to me back then, that this was a car fit for kings. So, as you can imagine, it was an enormous treat to be invited to ride in it with my grandfather every Saturday morning.

Our weekly outings were an extravagance I looked forward to eagerly, but for my grandfather, it signified something far more important. He was a fair man who had few rules and restrictions, but one thing he insisted upon was humility.

"Just because you are at the top of the tree, John, it doesn't mean you can forget your roots," he would say, looking down at me, kindly.

When I think of him now, I recall those wonderful lines of Kipling's: 'If you can talk with crowds and keep your virtue, or walk with kings—nor lose the common touch . . . Yours is the earth and everything that's in it.'

This summed him up perfectly, and it is why, after his chauffeur had polished the car and made it ready, my grandfather and I would ride together to visit his current building site. When we got there, he would get out and walk over to the men who were hard at work resurfacing the road. They would all sit down for their break together, my grandfather drinking his tea out of one of their mugs, genuinely eager to discover how their day had been.

It was on those treasured occasions that I learnt what it meant to be a leader of men. Watching my grandfather laugh and joke with his employees made me realise how important it was to treat everyone equally and I vowed to always follow his example.

I was learning the same valuable lessons at school, where my headmaster liked to repeat his favourite motto to us boys, in the hope that we would all grow-up to become gentlemen of honour someday.

"Manners cost so little, but mean so much," he would say to us, and we nodded, solemnly, understanding even at that young age the weight of what we were being told.

I may have lost my father to the war, but I was still luckier than most in that I had these two exceptional men to guide me through my formative years, and I was hugely grateful to them both.

Anyone who has spent the first few years of their life in constant fear and uncertainty, as I had, will know that it is not easy to believe in peace. So although peace had already arrived, I took my time accepting it. I still stayed awake most nights, listening out for the sirens to sound and I often woke in a cold sweat, imagining that I was cramped into one of our air raid shelters.

It seemed that England was also taking her time to adjust, and some things stayed the same for a long time after the war. We still had ration books and had to make do with scarce supplies of food, books, fuel and clothes. Not like now where you can go to a supermarket and buy almost anything you need at the drop of a hat.

Despite his good fortune, my grandfather still had to scrounge leftover cuts of meat from the butchers like everyone else, and we were always low on petrol tokens. But we did have one rather special secret weapon which made all this, somehow bearable—Pilar.

As a young boy, I was full of wonder for those who could create things I could not. My father's aluminium Lancaster Bombers were a marvel to me for this reason, and so was Pillar's cooking. All day long she would prepare her delightful concoctions out of what little we had, labouring diligently at the large pine worktable in the kitchen.

My grandparents had one of those marvellous old kitchens you often see in stately homes with a huge, cast iron stove in the centre providing warmth and exuding that comforting, homely feel all good kitchens ought to have. The ovens were either side of the fireplace and there was a hot plate on top for boiling a kettle.

I loved being in there with Pilar and was not at all surprised to learn that she treated her ingredients with the same respect and gentle devotion that my grandfather showed his employees.

Sitting, cross-legged by the stove, I watched, keen to learn, as Pillar heated pots of broth and rolled pastry for pies, making good use of our own vegetables and chickens to turn our scant provisions into hearty meals.

For a while, life proceeded at a regular pace and I was beginning, slowly, to enjoy myself. I still met regularly with my mother and younger siblings and we all chatted happily together, each revelling in those few, precious hours when we could forget the hardships of the last few years. I enjoyed school, too, and had earned a place as a left-winger on the football team. Something about the camaraderie of the sport appealed to my natural sense of team spirit, and of course, it was nice to feel the pat of a team-mate's hand on my back after a good goal. When I was old enough, I joined the school's Royal Air Corps cadets, but I didn't particularly relish the idea of making a career out of it—I was much keener on finding ways of forgetting the war than reminding myself of it.

Gradually, I came to think less and less of the air raids and the rubble and of my father flying Lancaster's over some foreign, faraway land. I was no longer that scared little boy who so desperately used to wish for morning, at the same time fearing what it might bring. Instead, under my grandfather's steady guidance, I was slowly becoming a young man. I had even developed a close friendship with a girl who lived up the road and we would see each other as much as time allowed.

I found I had a natural talent for learning and sailed through my exams with little effort, but despite my impressive grades, I still had one thing on my mind above all others—cooking. I had decided that I wanted to be a chef and fully intended to pursue my chosen career after matriculating. I had always enjoyed a harmonious relationship with my grandfather, so I wasn't especially nervous about telling him of my plans—which is why it came as an enormous shock when he objected, fiercely.

"You didn't go to a good school and pass your exams to become a chef, John!" he said, in that direct, yet fair way of his which made him impossible to contradict. "There is a whole world of opportunity out there and I expect to see you take advantage of it."

I listened to him then, as I always had, and took his advice, although I couldn't help feeling a little disappointed that things were not going entirely my way. Fortunately, however, my loyalty paid off and, together with my good academic reports and my grandfather's impressive business connections, I managed to secure an apprenticeship with British Transport Hotels as a trainee manager. I didn't know it yet, but this had been a generous and ingenious suggestion on my grandfather's part, as he no doubt knew that a large portion of my training would take place in the kitchens. I was thrilled when I found out. Not only was I on course for a good career, but I would be allowed to cook too! Life was, at last, a joy.

At that time, British Transport Hotels included some of the country's most prestigious establishments, and I began my training at the Queen's Hotel in Birmingham. I can remember that first day as if it were yesterday. It reminded me so much of my first day of school, standing tall in my new uniform, yet feeling terribly small inside. I missed my father dreadfully then. Having him there to reassure me and wish me well would have made it all seem far less daunting.

The first thing I noticed about the Queen's were the kitchens, which were pokey and awfully dark, as they were situated under the hotel—nothing like the vast, open space I was used to at my grandparents' house. Still, it was only a beginning, I told myself, and I was determined to do my best and prove to myself and my family that I could make a success of my career.

Professional kitchens are nothing like domestic ones. For one thing, they are absolutely terrifying! Not the warm, nurturing places most of us grow up with. Here, chefs bark orders at you from all directions; there are plates of food on every work surface, all at various different stages of preparation, and it appears that everything functions in complete chaos, when in fact there is an almost military precision to it all. It took me a little while to get used to the routine, but I was smart and eager to learn and soon got the hang of things.

I had never lacked confidence in my abilities, and before long, I thought myself capable of any task assigned to me; until, that is, I was asked to cook a piece of liver. The kitchens at the Queen's all had coal-burning ovens which had to be regularly topped up. This made it quite difficult to accurately judge their temperature, and on this occasion, I must have overdone it a little. Before long, the fiery heat, combined with the smell of the liver overwhelmed me and I fainted, unceremoniously, onto the kitchen floor. Not a very auspicious start, and I was reminded of it for quite some time afterwards by my amused colleagues.

I had only been at the hotel a few months, when I overheard one of the kitchen-hands talking about Gleneagles. I was already aware of its impressive reputation and knew that it was not only a hotel of exceptionally high standards, but also a favourite holiday destination for society's rich and famous, who flocked there every summer for the golfing season. I asked the boy if he knew anyone who had worked there and he told me that several people from the Queen's had already applied for transfers for the summer months. I was itching for a little adventure myself, so I put my name forward, not imagining for a moment that I would be considered, but to my enormous surprise and great delight, my application was accepted.

As I packed my case and prepared myself for the journey up to Scotland, I was reminded of the time my parents and I had moved to Stratford. I was certainly no stranger to change and yet I found myself worrying that I was making a big mistake—risking so much and heading, once again, into the unknown.

Chapter 4

Gleneagles

As it turned out, I had nothing to worry about—Gleneagles was a dream come true. It was everything I had expected a truly grand hotel would be, and as I stood before the main gates and looked at the impressive sight before me, I could see why it was sometimes known as the 'eighth wonder of the world'.

The grounds were, of course, spectacular and the hotel boasted two world-class restaurants and a buffet which was something of a legend in the hotel world. This bore no resemblance to the unimaginative tables of coronation chicken and limp samosas you so often get in holiday resorts or on cruise ships. Instead, there were cascades of fresh prawns tumbling down beautifully sculpted ice mountains and joints decorated to look like flamboyant peacocks and fairytale castles—all sealed in gelatine and nestled on beds of fresh, seasonal vegetables. I gazed at the displays, hoping desperately that I would one day be allowed to help prepare such glorious food art. What a long way we had all come from our war-time ration books and powdered eggs!

At Gleneagles, the kitchens were vast and divided into various different sections. Everything seemed to have been created on a grand scale—from the huge, walk-in fridges to the vast coal-burning ovens. I have to admit, it was all a little overwhelming and I was reminded of my first day of high school—with a stomach-full of butterflies and an overriding desire to crawl under a rock and hide.

The main kitchen had a glass roof to it, which allowed some of the smoke and fumes to escape when open, but there were still times— particularly on busy lunch shifts—when I found the heat in there quite unbearable. It was always a relief when my work was done and I could duck outside to breathe in the crisp, icy Scottish air.

I began my apprenticeship in the larder, under the watchful eye of a 70-year-old Frenchman named Michel Lebarb—one of the greatest chefs of the day and a true innovator. I still count his lobster with three sauces amongst my favourite dishes. I was told that the recipes he created were to be guarded with the utmost secrecy, which seemed ridiculous to me at first, but I soon learnt that other hotels often sent spies into our restaurant to discover the secrets of our much-coveted creations, so I had to be on my guard at all times.

It was a tremendous privilege to work with Monsieur Lebarb, even if he did box my ears with his rolled up copy of Le Monde when I wasn't paying attention. His meticulous attention to detail and natural flair made him an extraordinary chef to shadow and I had much to learn.

Above all, he was generous to a fault and keen to share his vast knowledge with me, something which set him apart from other chefs of his calibre. I watched his every move and listened carefully when he instructed me on the importance of timing and accuracy.

"A second too long on the heat and a sauce is spoiled," he would say with a knowing smile. Within just three months, this hugely experienced man had grown to like me so much, he treated me like a grandson. It was the greatest of honours and I thanked him by spending my breaks and spare time standing at his side, watching him work, hoping some of his genius would rub off on me.

Life in a busy kitchen is exhilarating and there is rarely a dull moment, which is probably why I loved it so much. In many ways, I felt like a young soldier—ready with a mop to clean up any spillages, listening out for the constant barrage of orders and all too aware of the consequences even minor mistakes would carry.

The noise was constant and ran through those vast, open-plan rooms like a pulse, beating to its own, relentless rhythm; but above the desperate calls for ingredients, shouts of occasional panic and food orders which blared out from loud-speakers in French, there was one word which always seemed to rise above the rest: "COAL!"

I soon discovered that whichever section I happened to be assigned to, it was essential that I had a good understanding of how the coal ovens worked. This, like most things at Gleneagles, took some getting used to. The ovens themselves were solid range cookers and each one had to be kept at a different and very precise temperature, which meant that we were all calling out to our poor, overworked coal man day and night—hollering at him to feed our cookers. His was a precision job—one minor miscalculation could ruin a dish which had taken several chefs some time to prepare. I certainly made my fair share of mistakes along the way, but once I had the hang of it, it became second nature and I quite enjoyed it. It was either that or get on the wrong side of the head chef—something I was not brave enough to do.

Anyone who has ever worked in a professional kitchen will know that the head chef is King—his orders are to be obeyed at all times and anyone who crosses him will suffer the consequences. Ours was no exception. Big Tom, as he was affectionately known, was a commanding presence, both feared and respected. At 6ft 6, he towered above most of us young, skinny apprentices and I soon learnt that I would have to follow all his instructions quickly and efficiently if I wanted to ensure a harmonious working environment.

After a little while, I progressed to the hors d'oeuvres section, where it was my job to make up the trolleys. It was a fun discipline, and as I painstakingly preparing trays of devilled eggs and liverwurst in gelatine, I thought fondly of Pilar and how I owed so much of this to her.

I was truly in my element, but there was trouble on the horizon. One of the kitchen boys didn't seem to think I was up to the job—either that or he was a little afraid I would threaten his position in the intricate hierarchy of kitchen life. It was a new experience for me, since I was an amiable sort of chap who usually made friends, not enemies, but we just did not see eye to eye, and one day, after several weeks of snide remarks and whispered insults, I decided to play a rather mean trick on him.

"Peter!" I said, calling him over to my corner of the kitchen. "I've got something for you to try. It's a luxury new vegetable—just arrived."

There was nothing to arouse his suspicions in that, as we received daily deliveries of fresh vegetables. Then I handed him an eye-wateringly hot red chilli and held my breath as he took it from me.

"What's it like, then, this luxury vegetable?" he asked, rightfully suspicious of my unexpected attempt at friendship.

"It's . . ." I struggled to find a description which wouldn't involve too big a lie. I had, after all, been brought up with good manners and did not wholly trust my ability to convince him of something clearly not true. "It's got a good, strong flavour," was all I could manage, but it seemed to do the trick.

Peter examined the chilli, briefly, before unwisely popping the whole thing in his mouth and chewing. It took a second or two for his senses to catch up with this terrible affront, then I saw his face contort into a wild grimace and he began to hop from foot to foot, waving his hand in front of his mouth as though it were on fire, which I suppose it was. I tried hard to suppress my giggles, but failed miserably and then Peter screamed, signalling the start of a monumental kitchen brawl.

Needless to say, I had a fair bit of dodging to do, as he reached out several times to grab hold of me, no doubt to tell me exactly what he thought of my luxury vegetable. I ducked and dodged, imagining myself once more on the school football pitch and was pleased with my success in avoiding a well-deserved hiding, but what we had both forgotten was that this was not our kitchen—it belonged to Big Tom.

I stopped in my tracks as our boss approached—wisely bowing my head in disgrace, but Peter was too mad by then to follow suit and continued to thrash about, oblivious to the danger he was in.

"What the hell is going on here?" Tom's voice was measured and icy cold, like the air outside, but I knew it was just the calm before the storm. Unamused by his childish tantrum, Tom picked the poor boy up by the scruff of his neck and dropped him into the fish tank—which was, at the time, full of live fish.

The maitre d' heard the ruckus and came to see what was happening, whereupon Big Tom, his blood well and truly up by now, threw a bucket of water over his head, thus initiating a rather comical scene. Before long, there was water everywhere, pots were upturned and smaller items hurled through the air to the accompaniment of angry shouts and bemused cries. It was carnage and a clear lesson to us all—cross Big Tom at your peril.

I stayed perfectly still, glad to have been spared any actual physical harm, but as I looked at Peter, drenched, his cheeks red with exertion and rage, I knew that I would have to watch my back from now on!

I kept my head down after that and worked hard, keen to avoid the fish tank and Big Tom's wrath. Before long, I had made a few, good friends and was beginning to settle into life at Gleneagles.

During my apprenticeship, I learned how to cook every conceivable joint of meat, how to fillet and prepare every kind of fresh fish, how to arrange those prawns on their various ice sculptures for the buffet and create wonderful sauces and vegetable dishes. I am quite sure I worked harder in my time there than I had done in all my school years put together and yet I enjoyed it tremendously, as much for the variety as for the stories it would provide me with. As a consequence, I am never short of a good anecdote or two from my time there.

Known for its excellent golf courses and a popular spot for shooting parties, Gleneagles had a regular clientele of celebrities, royals and world leaders and my job as a trainee manager was to learn how to cater to their every need. Usually, this meant knowing how to address each guest and being able to anticipate their needs. A good host always offers his guest a drink before they even know they want one. But my devotion to my trade was put to the test during a visit from the Nawab of Bhopal.

The Nawab was a much loved, politically astute leader and an excellent golfer and huntsman. Each year, he would visit Gleneagles during the shooting season, bringing an entourage of 40 people with him, a fleet of cars and his own chef—which was almost unheard of at Gleneagles. Very few people would have been allowed to bring their own kitchen staff, but he was a distinguished client, and being a Muslim, he had fairly strict dietary needs. For one thing, all the meat he ate had to be Halal, and prepared in a very specific way, and being rather junior, I was given the unpalatable task of killing the chickens for his specially prepared dishes.

Prior to this, I had always been rather proud of my robust constitution. I had no qualms about chopping large slabs of bloodied meat and wasn't squeamish about dropping live lobsters into a pot of boiling water for Monsieur Lebarb, but this would test even my hardy stomach. I had to first kill them, by breaking their necks, then cut off their heads and hang them upside down to bleed to death. I had grown up with chickens, but had never seen one killed before and it was something that would haunt me for some time afterwards. But I knew I could not complain, because disappointing the Nawab or, indeed, Big Tom, was not an option.

Aside from my rather unsavoury chicken-culling duties, I also had to spend a good deal of my time making people happy—whether the guests or the senior staff. I understood that to succeed at Gleneagles would take tenacity, talent and the ability to think fast on my feet. I was forced to put this to the test on many occasions, but still found it a little challenging at times and can only assume that my success there was as much to do with luck as it was skill of any kind.

There were too many heart-stopping moments to count—times when guests had been served the wrong dish, or shown to someone else's room. Not occurring with regularity, but when they did—boy, was there Hell to pay! Still, I liked to think I was a bit of a charmer. I had certainly inherited my grandfather's charm and was quite comfortable exchanging pleasantries with the distinguished guests, which is just as well because sometimes I was required to keep them talking a little longer than they might have liked.

One of those times was during a visit from Princess Alexandra [of Kent]. She was a regular guest at the hotel and always treated with the utmost care and attention. On this occasion, she had come up to the buffet to discuss her menu with myself and the head chef. She was just about to take her leave of us, when I spotted one of the apprentices gesturing wildly in the background. I assumed that something unplanned must have occurred and decided to stall our royal guest a little while longer. This was a pleasant task, yet even she could only be polite and courteous for so long. She was clearly keen to go and I had little option but to let her.

Later on, I discovered that the maître d' had been under the impression that she would be dining out that day, so he had allocated her usual table—in a well-positioned alcove overlooking the gardens—to another party. Upon realizing that she in fact had every intention of eating in, he grew concerned and needed time to relocate the other guests. With our hearts pounding, we followed her royal highness down to the restaurant and were hugely relieved to see that her table was free. The other party had to be offered a free lunch for the inconvenience, but it was a small price to pay and taught us all a valuable lesson: never assume anything.

The work at Gleneagles was often hot, tiring and always relentless, but there was fun to be had too. I was, after all, young and spirited and fully intended to enjoy myself wherever possible. I was lucky enough to have been given a room in the hotel not in the staff quarters, close to that of a young lad about the same age as me, called Colin. He was a smart fellow who shared my natural lust for life and we soon became firm friends, despite his penchant for winning all my hard-earned money in our regular, nocturnal card games.

"It's just a bit of fun, John," he would say, as he dealt me a hand, but several hours later and a few bob down, I realised that this was anything but fun. I enjoyed those games, more for the company than anything else, but learnt a valuable lesson, and to this day, I refuse to gamble—even on the horses.

Our rooms were more than adequate for our needs and we each had a fire, which was fine most of the year, but come February we both longed for something a little more effective to fortify ourselves against the harsh, Scottish winter.

The guests had their rooms below us and would leave their coal scuttles outside their doors each night in order to be filled, so Colin and I, in the spirit of Boy's Own storybook heroes, would creep down late at night and pinch a few pieces of coal for our rooms from the different scuttles. It did the trick and we miraculously never got caught.

One of Colin's main passions was football and we both took part in the friendly matches which provided regular diversion for the hotel staff. On one occasion, fired up and keen to score a goal, Colin took a nasty fall and hurt his ankle.

"I think it's broken, John," he whimpered and so I went with him to the local hospital. It was more of a friendly, rural cottage with some medical equipment than any hospital I had ever seen, but they did a good job and sent us on our way that evening.

Colin had a girlfriend, Anne, who lived in Rugby and I thought it would cheer him up no end if she would come and visit him in his hour of need. The only problem was that guests, especially female ones, were strictly forbidden. This, naturally, did not deter me, so I arranged to smuggle her in late at night and escort her to Colin's room without anyone noticing. I was, naturally, a little nervous and yet somehow, we managed. Anne was grateful to have the opportunity to nurse Colin for the evening and he was jolly pleased for the attention.

In the morning, Anne had to creep downstairs early before breakfast was started and leave unnoticed. Colin was grateful to me for my efforts and I was grateful not to have been caught out, as I'm not sure how kindly our managers would have taken to our French-farce antics.

Aside from my occasional schoolboy pranks, life at Gleneagles consisted largely of early mornings, late nights and a fairly relentless workload, so any free time I had, I made sure I enjoyed. There were a few perks that brightened up our moods no end and the greatest of these was that we were allowed access to the fabulous queen's golf course. The only problem, for most of the staff, was arranging transport down there, which is why I suddenly became rather popular. My stepfather had given me an old yet perfectly functional Vespa which I decided to take up to Scotland with me. I, unlike most of the staff there, had wheels!

To most, the Vespa is a very pleasant way to get around for one or two people—but I had to transport four of us, every day. I had made some good friends among the hotel staff and wasn't the sort of chap to leave anyone out. I was the driver, so naturally, I sat on the driver's seat with Colin behind me because he was the heaviest. Our diminutive friend, little Scottie, stood on the platform between me and the handle bars and the fourth in our party, Brian, sat on the back spare wheel of the scooter. Like this, we rode whooping with boyish delight and attracting a fair bit of attention along the way from people who marvelled at our ingenious circus act. We had a few bumpy rides, but it did the trick and we also enjoyed many good games on that world-class course.

After a few years of this precarious balancing act, Brian and I decided to take action and buy motor cars. Brian bought a sensible little Austin which stood him in good stead and proved reassuringly reliable. I, on the other hand, allowed Colin to persuade me to purchase a Ford Special which was no ordinary car.

"You won't regret it, John," he said, with a wink. "You're not the sort of chap for an Austin."

He was right, of course. I did want something a little more impressive, but this would test even my adventurous spirit. It had a powerful Ford engine built into the chassis and a wooden body. The roof was made of canvas and had little metal bars running along its width to enable you to take it off in summer. It was somewhat temperamental in starting, and I had a little oil can—the kind you press with your thumb to operate—with which I filled it with petrol. I had to time it just right—fill the carburettor, start the engine immediately, scare everyone no end with an impressive backfire and then off I went, as smooth as anything and jolly proud of myself.

Generally speaking, I was pleased with my little car, until one time when I had parked it in the hotel garage, along with the usual selection of impressive client cars. Somehow, it failed to start when I put the petrol in and instead, ignited. I stared at it for a moment, before breaking into a cold sweat.

"Fire," I whispered, at first. Then louder: "FIRE!"

I imagined how fast the flames would spread, not only through my little car but through the fleets of luxury motors belonging to wealthy clients, and saw my whole career flash before my eyes. There was absolute pandemonium as myself and some willing helpers struggled to contain and put out the fire. Fortunately we managed, but I never regarded that little Ford in quite the same light after that.

It nearly got me into trouble a second time, too—although on this occasion, I was rather more to blame. I had managed to secure a precious week's holiday, which I intended to spend by the coast, and for which I needed to catch a train straight after my last shift. Unfortunately, as was often the case, I didn't manage to leave the kitchen on time and was rushing around like a headless chicken trying to organize myself. It became clear that I wouldn't have time to catch the staff bus down to the train station, so I decided instead to drive myself there. I jumped in my car, started her up and went racing down the front drive, which was strictly forbidden for staff members.

There were two huge gates at the entrance to the hotel which were always left open and directly in front of them was a rather splendid roundabout—decorated with a striking display of roses. In my hurry and youthful carelessness I drove right through it and careered down the road in order to make it to the station on time.

I had a wonderful holiday and thought nothing of my behaviour until my return, when all hell broke loose. I was called directly to the general manager's office and given an unceremonious dressing-down. Being the owner of a beautiful Bentley himself, he gave me a much-heeded piece of advice: "Install a handbrake on your motor car, or don't bother coming back."

Needless to say, I took greater care when driving that old Ford and managed somehow to complete my memorable apprenticeship without any further dramas.

It seems funny now, reflecting on my life and the lives of those close to me, that less than two decades after losing my father to the war, I was preparing lobster for the rich and famous and balancing four on a scooter to play a round of golf on one of the best courses in the world, but that was how my life seemed to dip and dive.

One thing was for sure—I was having one hell of a ride!

After Gleneagles

I'd finally finished at Gleneagles, and was now fully qualified to enter into hotel management. After training at the auspicious Gleneagles, I had to give very careful consideration to any moves I made in my career progress, because starting in a hotel too low down the scale would be a retrograde step. It's very easy to slip down in the hierarchy of hotels, but very hard to climb back up again. Neither did I want to continue with British Transport Hotels, as it's not good policy to train there in a junior capacity, then take a managerial role in the same hotels. You end up managing people who have trained you, and there's always a sense of discomfort or even resentment with that, amongst the staff.

So, eager to do what I'd been training for at last, I set out to look for another job in a good quality hotel, and in due course I found a post at the Cairn Hotel in Harrogate. It belonged to the Forte empire, and was a beautiful, 4-star conference hotel. The hotel trade in Harrogate survived on conferences and trade shows, as well as people coming on holiday to Yorkshire, so the Cairn was well-placed.

So, after two interviews which seemed to go swimmingly, John Gordon, the manager, offered me the post. I was over the moon! I remember that I had to go and buy my first pinstripe suit—really feeling that I was management at last! The first day I started work there, I must admit that I was as nervous as hell to be in the role of assistant manager of this lovely, big hotel. There were two of us assistant managers—Martin, who had started some time before me, and me. John Gordon was the general manager, and of course, there were also the heads of departments.

There was the day-to-day job of being an assistant manager, which I was still learning, and I made mistakes, of course, but nothing really dramatic happened. One day when I was on duty, we had an extremely large conference in the hotel, and the breakfast had been particularly chaotic; not at all giving the right sort of impression that we hoped to display to our clients. I was very disappointed by the way it had been run, to say the least, so I went round individually to the head chef, the restaurant manager, and the housekeeper, expressing my concerns in the most serious of manner, and, to be honest—giving them a piece of my mind.

"Frankly, it was a shambles," I told the restaurant manager, whose face had reddened in rage throughout our conversation. "I don't expect this of our staff, and I don't expect it of you. Please see that it doesn't happen again."

With that, I turned on my heel and marched out, pleased that my pinstripe suit had done the job of boosting my self-esteem, and helped me to manage staff who were twice my age, with ten times my experience.

Oh, the foolishness of youth!

I thought nothing more about it until the afternoon, when John Gordon called me into his office. He was standing in the centre of the room, rather than sitting at his desk as usual, with his hands haughtily behind his back—something like a headmaster preparing himself to cane a recalcitrant pupil.

He said to me, "Mawdsley, you can take that chair," and he nodded towards his own seat behind the large oak desk, as he continued, " . . .

since it seems as though you think yourself a better general manager than me."

I gulped in surprise, but of course, recognizing his sarcastic intent, didn't take him up on his offer and remained standing, wide-eyed, as he continued.

"Congratulations. You have nearly lost your head chef, your restaurant manager and your housekeeper—all in one day. And so, if you think you can run the hotel all by yourself, without this calibre of experienced staff, you will be brilliant."

I swallowed hard, recognizing that silence was the best policy under these circumstances. *Listen and learn!*

"I hear that you have taken to hauling the heads of department across the carpet in no uncertain terms, and in a most arrogant tone."

I felt quite light-headed with anxiety, my throat too dry to respond even if I'd wanted to.

He continued, "Your high-handed treatment of these essential and highly experienced staff have caused quite a problem for me, and I have found myself having to smooth the ruffled feathers of all three departmental managers . . ."

And it was all my fault. Finally, John Gordon finished. "So I think you'd better go away and think of the repercussions that you've caused today."

Closing the door softly behind me, I duly did. Of course, I realised the error of my ways and had to go round apologising to each of the people I had inadvertently offended, eating humble pie. But at least I did it. It taught me a valuable lesson in humility and respect for experienced people and their areas of expertise. And after that, I even managed to become friends with the ladies and gentlemen who ran their departments so directly and efficiently.

Years later, when I had two or three hotels of my own, I realised that a hotel can easily run without a general manager for a short period of time as long it has strong heads of departments. However, it doesn't work the other way around: a hotel manager can't manage a hotel by himself. No hotel can run without its departmental leaders, because the whole heart of the business will just collapse. As a young and inexperienced assistant manager, I had believed in my own self-importance, thinking myself indispensable—only to find that I was sadly mistaken!

A few odd things that I remember about my time at The Cairn are worth mentioning. The Toy Fair annually booked all the hotels, big and small, in Harrogate to use for exhibitions, depending on the size of the company and the budget they were willing to spend. It was the most profitable period of the year for us.

To our delight and honour, Her Royal Highness Princess Margaret was coming to open the Toy Fair at our hotel, and all was primped and primed in readiness. Naturally, we had ensured that everything was in perfect order for our most illustrious royal visitor—and for the media attention we would attract from this honour.

The door to my office was at the back, not far from the entrance to one of the leading exhibition rooms, and an hour before Her Royal Highness was due to arrive, I was suddenly jerked from my reverie over the books in my office by a strange odour. It took me a few moments to identify as the smell of a wood fire, although I knew there were none around. I frowned in puzzlement, and my nose twitched involuntarily. Was I imagining it? No. I was fairly sure. I became aware that I could definitely smell smoke. So, concerned and curious, I went to investigate, peering out of my doorway. To my amazement, I spotted a haze of billowing smoke down the hallway—which I followed to its crackling source, only to realize that there was a blaze of flames engulfing the back stairs of the hotel!

I raised the alarm immediately, and the Fire Brigade responded within a matter of minutes. They were marvellous—they got it all quickly under control, with no harm done, apart from drenched and charred stair carpet and a sooty wall. Luckily, not in a visible public area of the hotel, so we were able to contain the damage.

But then, of course, we had this dilemma of a member of the royal family coming to open the Toy Fair, when the hotel fire had just been set on fire. With a frenzied phone call and some to-ings and fro-ings with the royal security service, it was decided that this breach of security should be taken seriously. We delayed the royal visit and managed to get away with the official opening of the Toy Fair otherwise running seamlessly, as if nothing had happened. Luckily, hardly anybody knew about our conflagration behind the scenes. Like swans gliding calmly on the still surface of water, we retained our appearance of sophisticated ease, and no-one was aware of the frenzy of furious paddling feet, and the murky weeds entangling us beneath.

After a little investigation, the fire was deemed to be arson: the person who had caused it had a maniacal hatred of the royal family and would set about doing all he could to disrupt them; but he was caught, fortunately—and out of the way, so we could relax.

Harrogate is well known as a spa town, and The Cairn itself had its own pump room and fully-equipped Turkish baths with pool, steam rooms and all the required leisure facilities of a high quality hotel in such a town at that time. One night, Martin and I, with our girlfriends, decided to use the Turkish baths after hours, so we sneaked across and happily let ourselves in. After all, what was the point of helping to manage such facilities if you couldn't impress the girls? By that time of night, the place had been closed for some hours, so we turned the pool heater up to warm it faster, and spent an hour or so deliciously swimming in the blood-temperature water, basking in the warmth. After finishing, we toweled ourselves dry, dressed, and tidied everything up of course, so the place looked as if we hadn't even been there. Then we happily went away, laughing and chattering.

In the morning, we walked into a major row. We discovered that the manager of the Turkish bath was going crazy! The swimming pool was at some unbearable temperature and nobody could swim in the boiling water! We listened to the news with raised eyebrows. Silence again proved to be the best policy, along with our slightly shocked and appalled expressions. *How could anyone have done such a thing?* we sympathized.

Unbeknown to us, we had forgotten ourselves and left the heat on the night before, still set at 'very high', and overnight the place had grown as hot as Hades. On this occasion, for once, we managed to get away without being found out.

What I most remember about the Harrogate period was that I had my first steady girlfriend there: Kathleen, a Yorkshire lass, living not too far away. While I was there, she wanted me to learn to dance properly.

"You're joking," I said, hopefully.

"Oh, come on, John! It'll be fun!"

I felt such a fool, since dancing was girls' stuff and my two left feet had their own ideas and often went their own way, but I reluctantly agreed. We went along to dancing lessons twice a week, in the afternoon. And in fact, after I'd got over the fright and foolishness, I really began to enjoy it, until we reached the stage where we actually became very good at it.

Life was happy. I had a car, I had a good job, I had a girlfriend, and I even had a dance life. Very soon, all of those would be gone!

After I'd been at The Cairn for some time, John Gordon called me into his office late one evening, which was unusual for him. I searched my mind for things I might have recently done wrong to warrant this eventuality, but unusually, I came up with nothing.

He said, "Sit down, John. I just want to chat to you."

I froze. He wasn't a chatty man. Had I done something wrong?

"John," he said, folding his hands precisely on the desk before him, and taking a long in-breath. "I want to know what you want to do with your career, and where you think you are likely to go from here."

That seemed serious, so I responded honestly: "Well, one of the reasons I joined the Cairn was that it is owned by Trust House Forte. So my idea was that I would progress . . . to eventually be a manager of one of their hotels."

"Well," he said. "No, John."

This was it, then! I stared at him, expecting my marching orders for some misdemeanour I wasn't even aware of. Or a list of small things that had all accumulated into a sackable offence. Such as inadvertently boiling guests alive like lobsters, in the hotel swimming pool.

John continued, oblivious to my wild imaginings. "That's not really what I think you should be doing. You have come so far, and done so well, I think you need to go abroad to get some really top class credentials on your CV." I raised my eyebrows at this news, but he went on, "You can learn another language and you will also learn another way of running a hotel of the same calibre, or greater, than Gleneagles."

After I'd absorbed this information I replied, "Well, if you really think this is what I should do, I will take your advice."

So without any more ado, he picked up the phone and asked the switchboard to get hold of a gentleman called George Morran at the Plaza Hotel in Paris. Within a moment, he was speaking directly to George: "George, I have a young assistant manager here who has spent three years training with me. I would like him to go to Paris and gain some international experience. What can you do about it?"

George said, "Leave it with me."

I left the office, bemused, my head full of wonderment. My future lay in the hands of these two men, but I was happy to wait and see what happened. I'd learned enough of what it meant to defer to the greater experience of respected experts in the hotel business. I'd learned that their instincts were often right.

The next morning, George Marron was back on the phone to John Gordon, saying, "I can get your young man into the Georges V on the front desk."

Despite being an apparent drop in grade, from my having been an assistant manager, the illustriousness of the hotel and the opportunities it offered were too good to pass up. I would be on the front desk in the uniform of the Georges V, which meant swallow-cut tails and black tie for the morning, and white tie for the evening. Well, I was completely over the moon to be offered a place in such a fabulous hotel! And on the front desk—it was quite auspicious! The job was to receive the guests who had booked to stay with you, take the clients to the room, arrange for the porters to have their luggage brought up, and make them feel at home.

There I was at the Cairn Hotel, Harrogate, having been an assistant manager for the last three years in a nice, secure, comfortable job, with quite a nice girlfriend and a very good boss. Yet it was this very boss who was responsible for me packing my bags to leave this very good job, from which my next step would naturally have been to be manager of quite a good hotel. But John seemed to be absolutely adamant that I needed international experience.

So, there I was, on my way to Paris, to an unknown job, an unknown life and an unknown language—to a place where I knew no-one. So, you can see that whilst it seemed exciting on one hand, it was also with some trepidation and some sorrowful farewells that I took the plunge into this strange new world.

Arrival in Paris

I arrived at the Gare du Nord, and took a taxi to this illustrious, famous world-class hotel, the Georges V in Paris. I thought myself an extremely lucky person to have been given this post through a friendship between two hoteliers; it just goes to show that more is achieved through who you know than by what you know. I was stepping down a considerable degree in my role, because I would be only a receptionist at this wonderful hotel, having already spent eight years training to be a manager. That intensive length of time should mean the end of training for a doctor, never mind a hotelier—but I knew it would be a step in the right direction.

So anyway, I was well en route to the Georges V when I asked the taxi driver to pull up a bit beyond the front door, not to be too noticeable. After all, I was staff, not one of their celebrity guests. The bell boy came to collect my luggage, and the concierge came to meet me, as I explained that I had come to work on the front desk.

They very kindly said, "Well, take a seat and we'll telephone Monsieur Choplin. Monsieur Choplin is the general manager of the hotel, responsible for all aspects of the hotel behind the scenes."

One of his secretaries came down and I was taken to the office and introduced. The normal procedures were explained to me and Mr Choplin explained that, "Under normal circumstances, a position such as your post allows you to live in the hotel—in a staff room—for a month, whilst you find my own property."

I thought this was really rather good of them. So, after all these induction notes, I was shown to my room, my baggage came up, and I was given two days to settle in before I started work.

I spent those two days marveling at the wonder of the hotel itself, grinning inside with delight to think that I was already a part of it. And also, walking down the busy boulevards and the quieter tree-shaded streets, lined with cafes and bars, drinking in the atmosphere of Paris itself, which I loved initially, and which love would only grew deeper as the months passed.

On the morning of my first starting work, I met Monsieur Bonntot, the head of the brigade of receptionists which I was joining. He was to be my immediate boss throughout the time of me being there. His superiors were Monsieur le Mercier, Chef de Reception, and Monsieur du Pont, the hotel's general manager for the front of the hotel.

Monsieur du Pont had the most gorgeous office of all, all made of glass, alongside the desks the guests attended, where the reception staff worked. Therefore he could see everything and ensure that everyone was working well; with good visibility of the road and of anybody arriving through the front door. He had been at the hotel for close on thirty years, and was likely to retire before I left the hotel. He was adored by everybody, was a star to work with, and was known throughout the world by the hotel guests who stayed there, especially the rich and famous, of whom he made such a fuss.

So, I came down to start my work, in my very smart tails, and Michel and I went off to the lounge, where he started to explain my duties and the role.

"The sole purpose of reception is to make each and every customer feel welcome and looked after to the best of our ability whilst they are here. So, most of the time you are meeting and talking to your clients," said Michel. "The only paperwork you religiously must do is to make a detailed card index of each client who arrives, with every detail in respect of which room he stays in and what he likes; so that on their return visit you know exactly their past history."

Michel explained that my role was to take clients to the room and that I was allowed twenty to thirty minutes with each client, depending on their standing. If it was someone of exceptional note, Michel was to be immediately informed and either he or Monsieur le Mercier would then look after the client personally. But on a normal day it was the responsibility of me or whichever colleagues were available upon the arrival of a client, or to attend any client who came to the desk with an enquiry.

I was told that I would be permitted to speak, and they would speak to me, in English for the first three months; but from there on, I was expected to speak in French all the time that I was on duty. That might sound a bit forbidding, except for the fact that I'd decided from the very beginning that I would have a strategy to immerse myself wholly in the French experience. There were a number of English hotel staff who went out socializing together and never really met any French people, as they might perhaps have preferred. But I made the decision that I would only have French friends and speak only in French. So it became relatively easy to meet the roles and stipulations that Michel had set down. I made a lot of friends, primarily from work. Because I was only interested in speaking in French, it made an enormous difference to the French people's outlook and opinion of me—proving that I was really interested in France, the French people and the French friends I had met.

So, there I was, settled into the role that I was expected to carry out for as long as I could stay. I was on a work permit in those days, and I could only renew it once, normally; so your stay was really for a maximum of 18 months to two years, depending on which local government official decided to see your papers. I was determined to stay as long as I could.

I managed to find a very nice apartment with a lovely little living area, not far from the hotel, on the third floor in a very old building, as a lot of French apartments are. It was on the corner, so I was able to see out across the square one way or another, giving me a very pleasant outlook of the bustle of Paris below.

So, now that I was settled in my accommodation, doing shifts from eight till three or four, and from three till the end of the shift at eleven o'clock or midnight, I decided to obtain some sort of transport. Back in the 1960s, the modern day motorbikes and scooters did not exist. I purchased a mobylette—a bicycle with a motor on the front wheel, which was perfectly all right in dry weather, but of course, skidded like a surfboard in the wet. However, this was more than adequate for getting to and from work, and especially good for getting around Paris, because the traffic was not overly fast, even in those days. So I was able to get about, free of charge, relatively easily.

When I'd settled in, they trusted me to know how to handle a client, especially with my experience in both my past jobs, so I was soon allowed to see most of the guests on my own, depending on who it was, where and when. So really, the job was a bit of a doddle! Sometimes, especially if the guests were busy business executives, all they wanted was minimal contact, dismissing us with a "Thank you very much, that's all I need!" But we also had a tremendous number of tourists, particularly American, who liked much more of a fuss made of them. Only, of course, once you started chatting to them, they began to believe that you could be their personal guide for their entire holiday in the capital.

What I had not really expected in my initiation into the role was that I was expected to know Paris extremely well. But it was, of course, a pleasure to discover, and I successfully familiarized myself with Paris during the first three months so that I soon knew my way around. I was introduced to all the major fashion houses—Dior, Balenciaga, Lacroix, Yves St Laurent—and others in the haute-couture world, because that's what most of the ladies who came to stay with us wanted. The second thing guests wanted to know was a reliable restaurant. So I was taken around to be introduced by a colleague from our hotel, and I soon got to know the Maître d's of the best restaurants in Paris. You would explain who you were and where you came from, giving them the promise to send them business whenever possible. So, of course, this led to them looking after you exceedingly well, so that you either got cash back at the end of the month, or you had the value of eating in the restaurant for free whenever you wished. There was a two-fold purpose and mutual benefit, really, because I needed to know how to get clients a seat at the fashion houses and a table at the type of restaurant they requested, so I had to know the type of food served and the area of Paris they were located. For their part, the fashion houses and restaurants wanted the clientele from our hotel, because they knew that our wealthy clients' pockets were very well-lined. The same thing happened at the box office of the theatres, because all these people were clamouring for clients from the Georges V, knowing that they had lots of money to spend.

I had been well-briefed on my duties, and I accorded our clients all the attention I was allowed. On taking a guest to their room I had the freedom to speak to them for twenty minutes to half an hour, to make sure they were happy. Some of them knew Paris inside out, and all they requested was, for example, a table at the Lido for the late show, or a table at Maxim's at nine, and I simply had to arrange it. On the other hand, there were many, many clients who had never been to the city of Paris before, who really relied on our help.

For offering all this assistance while you were with clients, it seemed to be common practice that you were tipped. I'd been well taught by colleagues at the famous restaurants, fashion houses and major sight-seeing venues, so I was able to help guests with advice and information. The better you were at this job, the bigger the tip you received, so attention to detail proved to be most beneficial. Now, I'm talking about the late '50s, and if you were being tipped by Americans, to be honest, they didn't really know the value of the currency in France, so they tipped you in dollars; and it was very easy to obtain a $100 bill—that was nothing to an American client. And then, of course, when they went to the restaurants we recommended, the restaurateur kept a note of the clients we sent, and paid us a reward of some sort. We would build up benefits in kind, through free meals and tickets, or receive a monthly commission from them that went into the hotel trunk, like all the rest of the tips we received, and we later obtained our individual share—which was considerable—at the end of each month. So, you can see that this soon became an exceedingly well-paid job, considering that these additions were tax-free.

Despite the plethora of freebies, that was the first time in my life that I adopted a policy of not saving any money. I had made up my mind to spend what I had while I was there, and enjoy it.

One day, I happened to meet the gorgeous Sophia Loren, who was coming to stay at the hotel. She came to the Georges V very frequently, had many friends, and of course, there were many followers of this famous film star clamouring for her attention. She always knew exactly what she wanted and requested it confidently. Normally, Michel would have taken her to her suite, but since he was already with a client on this occasion, it fell to me. It was unusual for her to have an English person attending her, and she became very chatty. From then on in, each time she came, I had the pleasure of taking her to her suite. And I have to say what a delightful person she was, in her ordinary way, off-stage.

Her rival, Gina Lollobrigida—who was just as famous as Sophia Loren, particularly for her figure, but in a different way—was a frequent guest and I also took her to her suite. Again, she knew precisely what she wanted, but in contrast to Ms Loren, she was rather short and snappy and did not really become too friendly. Although I did see a lot of her—unexpectedly more than I ever anticipated, as you will discover.

Ironically, at the end of one visit, on her day of departure, Gina Lollobrigida had removed her things, checked out, paid the bill, vacated the room, and then, of course, it was cleaned in preparation for the next arrival.

I took a gentleman up to the room he was allocated to, and having no reason to knock at the door, I simply opened it and went in as usual, followed by the gentleman. I was about to ask him what he required, when lo and behold, the bathroom door opened and a naked, wet Gina Lollobrigida stepped out into the bedroom, showing off her famous figure more obviously than any of us would have anticipated.

Both the lady and gentleman gave embarrassed gasps, and stared at one another, mouths gaping, while I attempted to maintain my discretion and stiff upper lip.

Worse still, I presumed that the male client must know Gina Lollobrigida very well, since she was apparently waiting for him, naked. So I said, "I'm awfully sorry. I didn't know you were expecting a guest," and discreetly left the suite with great swiftness.

Well, gosh!

What we did not know was that Gina Lollobrigida had not handed her keys in at the desk. Unbeknown to us, she suddenly decided to return to 'her' apartment to have a shower. We soon became incontrovertibly aware of this.

Within a few minutes, the gentleman had followed me down to the reception office and was playing merry hell.

"What do you take me for?" he cried.

Why were we, the Georges V of all places, he demanded, taking him to a bedroom furnished with a naked woman? Even if it was a famous film star!

Merry hell was also let loose by my colleagues for months to come after that incident, and my leg was pulled continually. Mutterings about my offerings of 'room service' and the fact that I had tried to pimp out Gina Lollobrigida meant that I never lived it down.

These kinds of famous people or events never crossed my path in Gleneagles or Harrogate, which was, of course, rather a quiet, sleepy time in comparison. Paris was a bubbling world capital where the clientele came on business, often on expense accounts, and many far away from home. Lonely men with lots of money tend to attract a different sort of clientele.

The hotel was adamant that no prostitutes got into the hotel to their knowledge, and working girls were not allowed to patrol anywhere near the Georges V. In fact, I recall one occasion, when one girl had the audacity to do so, winking at our clients in a meaningful way as she strutted her stuff on the boulevard outside, and sneering at Michel's pointed glares and ineffectual flicks of the hand to usher her away. She pretended not to notice him, and merely lit a cigarette, pulling on it lasciviously with her red-painted lips.

Since his discreet attempts to send her on her way had failed, Michel was determined to take a more direct approach. He went in, got a bucket of water, came out of the front door, and marched towards her. With a mighty sweep, he flung the bucketful of water at her and soaked this girl. That stopped her smoking, and got her attention, too. Once she was able to open her eyes and cough up the mouthful of water she had inhaled, she swore at him vociferously, which helped to improve my French no end. We couldn't stop laughing. She stalked off, fuming, leaving a trail of water behind her. Of course, we never saw her again.

But nature is nature, and all the world over, men desire female company. Although we would never initiate a transaction, if a gentleman expressed an interest in some female company, it was our unwritten policy to provide our clients with almost anything they required—a level of customer services that some might say goes beyond the call of duty. So, we knew of quite a number of escort girls—who were extremely pleasant girls, very intelligent, very smart—whom we could recommend. If the client wished to go to a restaurant, theatre or even business meetings with a lady to accompany him, choosing a professional meant that he could do so with a pleasant companion, without being let down by her behaviour or attitude. Our role ended with the discreet passing on of the barest of information to each party concerned. Whether it was for company for the evening at the theatre, dinner or a show, and /or including bed, it was really up to him and the lady to negotiate the terms. And we, at the hotel, pretended not to know; although in fact, on most occasions we had asked them to come.

On my early morning shift, I usually came in on my mobylette and went to a little café to have my coffee and croissant before starting work. It might seem funny, but lo and behold, many of these very smart girls were in the same café as me, sitting by themselves, drinking coffee or having their breakfast in their evening gowns, furs and cocktail dresses, before going home to rest, I suppose. We would smile at one another, acknowledging that we were all professionals in the tourism and leisure industry. Gradually, I got to know them very well indeed, because they were something like regulars to the hotel, and by chatting and getting to know them, I came to understand their way of life. On the surface, it seemed so odd to be passing the time of day with them in a café, but while we never became close friends, we developed an amicable companionship over coffee and croissants. And they never charged me a fee for their pleasant company and chats across the formica tabletops.

Also frequenting the same café was another young lady who was very smartly dressed, often in the colours of the French flag, I noticed. One morning I decided to break the silence and go over and speak to her. I began by introducing myself—it was very informal—then we both went our separate ways. This subsequently happened a few times; I went and sat down and had my coffee and croissant with her, discovering that she worked for Air France. We just seemed to hit it off and like each other a lot. Her name was Marie-Claude, and I became quite fond her. In fact, you could say I was rather smitten. So she ended up being my girlfriend for all the time I was in France. She was great fun to go out with, and she also knew how good any of the top restaurants were, because of her own job as an air hostess. On many occasions, instead of going to the Lido or Maxim's or any other lovely restaurant bearing Michelin rosettes—where of course, I got meals free—we would just go out to a normal little bistro, Saint André or Saint Georges, very well-known little restaurants that served excellent food, not too far from where we lived.

I have to say, she was really very romantic and taught me the art of making love. It was really quite surprising, because I'd had girlfriends in England, but Marie-Claude was somehow quite different. Her being continental may well have been one of the reasons, but I didn't mind at all! We had great fun together, and when my time came to go, sometime in the future, I would be very sorry to leave her.

We both liked opera, and laughingly, I dressed up in my white tie and tails for the opening night of Tosca at the Paris Opera House, with Maria Callas. I was so pleased to have got tickets, which normally would not have been possible without our connections in the hotel. The funny thing was that I couldn't get a taxi at the time, so I got on my moped and tucked my tails underneath me, on my saddle. While the sight of me riding along with tails fluttering behind me in the wind might have cut more of a dash, I didn't fancy ending up like Isadora Duncan with my tail caught in my spokes. So, neatly tucked in, I drove off to the front doors of the Paris Opera House, chained my bicycle to the railings at the side of the building, smoothed my tails and my hair, and, debonair as ever, went up to meet Marie-Claude.

That night was never to be forgotten. The soaring arias and swell of the orchestra filled my heart, and the stunning atmosphere of the Paris Opera was the perfect environment for such a magical experience. Tosca has always remained one of my most beloved operas, and I always compare Maria Callas with the later divas who followed—although there is actually no comparison.

There was a lovely little cabaret bar near Café de la Pays, one of the most well-known coffee houses in Paris. Just a few doors away was this little cabaret club where we often went, because it was great fun. You could have a nice light meal down the road at the Café de la Pays and go on there, afterwards. Their star at the time, would you believe it, was Shirley Bassey—so no wonder we liked her, because in the years to come, we all know how famous she became. It is funny to look back on how often we went to see her in her early life in Paris, her broad Welsh accent as incongruous as the quality of her singing in that small, humble venue in the French capital.

I would sometimes have days off when I didn't know quite what to do, especially when Marie-Claude was away for a few days on a long-haul flight, so I did succumb to making friends with a guy called David Ward who had come over to the Plaza Athénée, which was a hotel of similar standing to the Georges V. Somehow when we met, I broke my rule of not befriending any English people, but we liked the idea of learning about French wines, a love which has stayed with me for the rest of my life. We went out, exploring the chateaux region of France, south-east of Paris. All the vineyards were famous for making Sancerre wine, so it was great fun examining the differences from one establishment to the next.

"Ahh," said David, his eyes closed contemplatively, rolling a mouthful of wine across his tongue. "A cheeky little 1948, grassy as a May meadow scattered with buttercups, with a soupcon of lemon verbena; born of chalky soil from the south-east . . . No . . . I tell a lie— the south-south-east foothills . . ."

We started without much of a clue, but our tongue-in-cheek approach developed into a more sophisticated taste and actual factual knowledge.

This got us interested in other wines, and on another week's holiday we went off down to Beaune, staying in B&Bs, and called on all the vineyards—some famous, some not so well-known. We were always greeted with enormous enthusiasm by wine afficianados, and so, little by little, we learned about the wines of the Loire and the wines of Beaune. David and I didn't go out socially at all, really, at any other time, apart from our wine trips.

As I mentioned, Marie-Claude might be flying on a long-haul flight and would be away for a couple of days, so when my shifts finished at three o'clock, I would usually explore Paris, delighting in wandering through characterful streets and along the Seine, where the booksellers plied their trade, or through the elegant galleries, and I'd buy things like blotting paper. I loved going down to the Left Bank, where all the students and young art lovers used to go to the cafés and little Italian restaurants, the soft sound of jazz leaving a trail like cigarette smoke on the streets, and I'd just drink in the atmosphere. It was just a quarter of Paris that was very different, with its two islands, and not far from Notre Dame. You could go there any day and find it totally different from the next, depending on the people who were around. Every day gave another subtle nuance of late and shade on the picture I had of Paris, ever-changing.

Getting to know how some of these artists worked, I was then drawn to Pigalle, which was an area of vast entertainment, buzzing with life, with artists galore in every conceivable medium; famous for the red light district, the Moulin Rouge and all the other nightclubs. It never failed to entertain you, and I've never found an atmosphere like it anywhere else in the world. I have always been attracted to it every time I have gone back to Paris numerous times over the years, later on when I was married. I can't help but go there with my wife.

Service Is Our Specialty!

Chapter 7

Venice

Whether wandering through the boulevards, the galleries or the parks, or simply sitting in cafes talking philosophy, I would have loved to stay in Paris. But in those days, one needed visas and work permits, and mine, unfortunately, had expired long ago. I was now clearly told that I had to leave France, and reluctantly, looked for a job in another exclusive hotel.

After a short spell, I secured a post at a hotel of the same standing as the Georges V and Gleneagles: the Royal Danieli in Venice, without doubt one of the finest hotels in existence.

During my time at Gleneagles, my weakest area—and one that I needed to address in order to succeed—was working in the restaurant. I managed to get a very desirable post at the Danieli, in the rooftop restaurant, secured through my experience at Gleneagles and Paris, and because of my skill in languages. I was given a job as chef de rang, controlling twelve tables in a restaurant. Once the head waiter had seated the clients, I would introduce myself and take their orders, and it was my job to look after the party to the best of the Danieli's capabilities. Each table might hold anywhere between two people or a party of twelve—whatever transpired on the day. The Danieli restaurant was so famous that it was extremely difficult to get a table, so once they'd secured one, clients really expected to be looked after extremely well. You'd never know who you were going to serve next. I met many famous business people and stars; all sorts of people who liked to dine out in good restaurants—as you can well imagine, I'm sure.

The food at Danieli was gourmet, par excellence. Having experienced kitchen training, I very well knew the stress they went through when harassed waiters screamed, "Where is my table's order? Why am I waiting?" So, for the waiters serving the tables, a little trick we learned was to not only take the client's order, but to memorise exactly who had ordered what, so we recognized the prepared order at the pass, and didn't have to ask the clients on the table which meal was which, either. It was part of the standard of the establishment—that the waiters were discreet and remarkably adept.

Unfortunately, the job was a split shift, which was very hard work because you came on at around half past ten in the morning, to make sure that your station was ready and to check bookings. Then you had to be ready for twelve noon, when the restaurant opened. Lunch carried on well up to 3.30pm, when the last client left. With any luck, by then you had cleared the other tables; but if not, you had to stay longer—then return at 6pm to be ready for 7 o'clock opening, after which you wouldn't finish until at least 11 o'clock! So as you can see, the days were fairly hard and long, with hardly any free time to take a break, let alone socialize or take leisure.

I managed to get a small apartment not too far away from the hotel, and having a bicycle made things a little easier, since you could ride alongside the canals quite well, and get around the small city quickly and easily. It also made life very interesting on your days off, to explore this absolutely wonderful city, so full of art, impressive buildings and museums; the narrow canals forming the streets and antique bridges giving Venice its particularly unique character. It was a sheer delight, because I had nothing else to do but enjoy and absorb all that Venice could offer. I had no girlfriends, just my work and the enjoyment of the city's well-known attractions, and more. And I have to say, once I was familiar with the usual tourist attractions, I found the buildings, their architecture and the history of the Venetians far more interesting, and I'd journey up the canals exploring the real Venice, far beyond where tourists would normally go. Although it was equal on all accounts to London and Paris, it was very different.

I didn't intend to spend as long in Venice as I did in Paris, because I'd already spent so many years training to be a manager that I was keen to make headway in my career. This was really a sort of top-up to my experience and knowledge, to hone my skills and ensure that I was really on the ball in a restaurant and could manage a kitchen if I had to.

I'd had it in my mind that I would return to England and hopefully get a job in a well-known London hotel in a managerial capacity. However, whilst I was in Venice, a most unexpected thing happened to me: one that I'd never dreamed would ever be possible.

I ended up obtaining a post with the royal household, in Clarence House, working for the Queen Mother.

A total change of direction

As much as you think you know London, you forget what a lovely city it happens to be. Whilst you can't compare London with Paris, because they have their own idiosyncrasies, London is very much a major, global capital city. It's just as historic as Paris—so there is a lot to learn. Just as I had to learn what Paris had to offer, I learnt what London could give.

My role at Clarence House was working for Her Majesty the Queen Mother directly, attending to her requirements in the days and months to come, and organising each day on her behalf. I couldn't believe that I had obtained such a post, but there you are! Well-used to looking after clients of the highest degree in both Paris and Gleneagles, I was totally confident in my role with the Queen Mother. However, the hotel world was like theatre; the royal household was totally different, run very much in a military style. This was all when Her Majesty was in her sixties and still very much full of life. One tends to remember Her Majesty in her frail, later years, but when I was with her she was very vibrant and a very busy lady, so you were very much kept on your toes. I was kitted out in the smartest of dress, for morning and evening, and for going out. Sometimes I might accompany Her Majesty down to Newmarket, sometimes to a private tea party, dinner party or some part of a state visit, so you had to be well-versed in the etiquette and procedures for all types of occasion.

I'm sorry, but I'm not going to go into any further detail about my time there, out of courtesy for Her Majesty. Her life was private and I'm not going to break any confidences or start telling stories, so you'll have to bear with me on that count.

Of course, that position had its perks and benefits, like those I received in Paris, to some degree. I was given a lovely little courtesy flat in Park Place, three quarters of the way up to St James's, on the left, behind the Ritz Hotel. I bought the most beautiful two and a half litre Riley motor car, which was a bit of a nuisance in town, but I went out quite a lot. I'll tell you more later.

I live in Chester now, and I didn't have that much contact with the North West before; but it's ironic, isn't it, life? I met two friends— Lawrence Nuttall, from Lancashire, and Jeffrey Thompson, from Blackpool. Both of them had recently graduated and were working in London at the same time as I arrived back from Italy. Lawrence worked for Plessey, the big international electronic company. Jeffrey was the son of the owner of Blackpool Pleasure Beach, and after he'd graduated from Cambridge University, his father had told him that he needed to gain some London experience, so he worked for a laundry company with a friend.

I can't remember how we all met, but we ended up rather like the three musketeers, becoming such good friends that we were almost inseparable. Funnily enough, we stayed like that for the next 40 years, when unfortunately, Lawrence committed suicide. This was a most dreadful shock to us all. Jeffrey and I were really distraught; being so close, if things had been so bad, we would have expected Lawrence to have said something about feeling so down—but he never showed it at all, with us. Just one day, it happened. It was a terrible shock to everyone— not least his family. I went to help look after his wife and son, who was at public school at the time, to offer them some support at the time.

Then, a few years later, Jeffrey died on the day of his daughter's wedding, during the celebrations. He was just about to make a speech to his daughter when he suddenly died, right there and then. So tragic! I found that very hard to bear.

I'll tell you more about that side of my life later on, because eventually I became a Director of Blackpool Pleasure Beach, but that's way to come, yet.

On one occasion, I was invited to a fancy dress event—a pyjama party, in fact. Always game for some fun, that evening I put on my newly-ironed striped winceyette pyjamas, jumped in the Riley, and sped off up towards Picadilly. Halfway to my destination, there was a great metallic clattering sound behind me, and I looked in my rear view mirror to see that my exhaust pipe had dropped off and was bouncing down Picadilly. *Damn!* But I was running late, and despite the terrific roaring sound of the engine with no silencer or exhaust, I drove on, hoping no-one would notice.

Just outside Fortnum and Mason, I was flagged down by the police. *Damn!* They had clearly noticed.

"Is this your car, Sir?" said the officer, eyeing my pyjama-jacket oddly.

"I'm afraid so," I apologized.

"Can I ask you to get out of the car, sir?"

"Of course you can ask, but I'm afraid I can't. You see, I'm wearing pyjamas . . ." I began, but was interrupted.

"Sleep-walking, were we, Sir?"

"Or sleep-driving?" added his colleague, with a smirk.

"I'm going to a fancy dress party, you see. That's why I'm in pyjamas, and that's why I can't get out. We're in the middle of Picadilly—it's a busy high street!"

"I'm very sorry, but I require you to get out of the car," he persisted.

I huffed out of the car and stood there in the middle of Picadilly in my Winceyette pyjamas and tartan slippers, my hands clasped in front of my fly-front, looking sheepish.

"Where do you work?"

"Clarence House."

The two policemen looked at one another and frowned. The first one smiled sarcastically, "'Course you do, Sir. And I'm the Queen Mother."

"Ahem," I smiled. "No, you're not. I should know. I work for her."

"Right," the second officer said, uncertainly. "Do you have any identification?"

I patted my pyjama top breast pocket, "Not on me. But hang on!"

I ducked back into the car and scrabbled in the glove compartment for my wallet and driving licence, and a work pass. I showed it to them, and the two officers raised their eyebrows, unable to believe their eyes.

"Have you been drinking, Sir?"

"Not yet. I'm just on my way TO the party, you see."

"Can I ask you to walk in a straight line, just here, please, sir?" the second officer said, waving his hand peremptorily towards a gap in the crowds on the pavement, who were gathering to watch the entertainment.

"Really?" I asked, "Is this quite necessary? Outside Fortnum and Mason's?"

"I'm afraid so, sir."

Summoning as much outraged indignation as a man in striped pyjamas on Picadilly outside Fortnum and Mason's could summon, I dutifully walked an imaginary tightrope on the pavement before them. The crowd gave a smattering of applause when I'd finished. I declined to bow.

"Thank you sir. That's fine," the police said, hardly able to hide their amusement. "Well, if you can promise to get this exhaust fixed as soon as possible tomorrow, we'll let you get on your way."

"Thank you," I said tightly, and began to get into the car.

"In future," the first officer said, confidentially, leaning in through the window, "Next time you're going to a fancy dress party, I'd take your outfit and get changed when you arrive there."

"I'll take your advice, officer," I said. "I'll go now, if that's all right with you."

The crowds waved me off, applauding, while my Riley set off with a jet engine roar, back-firing like a clown's car at the circus.

While I was in London, I met a girl called Anne, who was living in the same apartment as Lawrence's girlfriend, coincidentally. Anne came from Hereford, and was working in the hotel industry too, on the front desk as a receptionist. We became inseparable during the years I was in London and fell very much in love. Even when we'd been out all day with each other, no sooner would Anne get back home than we'd spend another hour on the telephone, chatting away as if we hadn't seen one another in months and had lots to catch up on. I understand where my daughter gets it from!

I could get a theatre seat or a table in any restaurant I wanted, because of my position, and if the royal box was not being used in Covent Garden I was allowed to have it for myself and friends. This occurred quite often, because the royal family only infrequently used it. So we saw some of the finest productions of opera and ballet, and that's really where I developed my sheer love of opera, for which I became passionate. It was also fairly customary for Anne and I to go to Windsor on Sundays to watch the polo, which we found great fun, especially driving in my Riley. We were accepted by the royal family, in a reserved way, if you can understand what I mean.

I got to know London; not as well as Paris, I suppose, but certainly very well, because Anne and I both liked to explore, and do things together. That period was enjoyable because of Anne in particular. It was the first time that I'd really fallen in love, and I fell hard.

Just before I left London to come to Chester, I took Anne for a short holiday in Paris and taking a risk I thought was fairly safe, I proposed to her, really wanting to marry her and settle down.

Unfortunately, or fortunately—one does not know in life—Anne turned me down. And of course, this was soul-destroying. I know it's happened to hundreds and hundreds of other people, but this was me—I had laid out my heart for her to take and she had refused. At the time it really upset me. I almost thought my world had come to an end. But of course, it was just beginning.

I spent four and a half happy years working at Clarence House, and I only left because I'd long desired my own establishment, and a chance came up with a small club in a Victorian mansion house in Chester. The Walker family from Bolton had backed me in buying this establishment, so now was my chance.

It always seems to take ages for lawyers to finalise the details of the purchase of a business. But anyway, after lots of negotiation, I was bound for Chester at last.

Purchase of hotel

Mollington Banastre was a club in a Victorian house built on top of an earlier building dating from the 1300s. We bought it from Mr and Mrs McFarlane, who'd run it as a country club, with 12 bedrooms. It was a country house, absolutely the most beautiful place—as you'll see from the photographs. I fell in love with it. It was one and a half miles from the city of Chester, set in its own countryside, amongst the farming community.

As an old Roman fortified city with some fine Tudor architecture, too, Chester itself was a magnet for tourism, which was one of my main criteria for somewhere to buy as a business. Chester was also very popular with businessmen, because it was only just over half an hour from Liverpool where there were no good hotels, and it wasn't so pleasant—so businessmen often stayed in Chester. I'd done my research, and believed that I had chosen the right formula for success.

So, by Christmas 1964, I took possession of my own business. And I can tell you, when I arrived, still in my Riley car, and walked through those doors, the feeling of trepidation that ran through my whole being is indescribable! I was no longer working for some big organization: the business was going to be run by me, the direction we went in was mine, the responsibility and whether we succeeded or failed would be mine. Some people might have thought I was crazy for buying this small, somewhat tatty establishment with no ratings, no stars, no nothing, after all my years of training in the most exclusive of cosmopolitan hotels. But I was just like a vet who spends eight years at university and suddenly finds that he's now a qualified vet with a practice to run and sick animals to cure, and clients with high expectations. It was all too real!

Christmas was a funny time to take over a business, really. I'd happily said goodbye to Mr and Mrs McFarlane, seeing them off the premises, and I'd met all the staff. To be honest, I thought they were a pretty ropy lot, and it disillusioned me somewhat. I would have to do something fast, I felt, to make my mark and instill the kind of standards I wanted. On the ground floor of this lovely Victorian English country house, the lounge was decorated in some kind of weird caricature of a Scottish theme, with thistles and bagpipes, salmon and stags, and novelty haggises, and the bar was horrendous. Dreadful! Clashing with the thistle-patterned wallpaper, there was tartan carpet everywhere, which I think Mr McFarlane pretended was his own tartan. The restaurant was in the middle of the house, overlooking these magnificent gardens and the rolling countryside, but the décor inside was enough to break your heart, and put you off your dinner. The wallpaper was black with spots all over it.

I'd seen it all a couple of times when I'd been up with Lawrence to look over the establishment before getting involved, so at least I knew what to expect; but nevertheless, it was pretty dreadful. The kitchens were reasonably well laid out, clean and reasonably kept. The person who ran it was not, but we'll come back to him later. We had a ballroom then, which I have to say, was a very good size. But its furnishings, again, were atrocious! The chairs were like school-room stacking chairs with metal frames. I nearly died, because having been used to some of the finest furnishings in the world, coming down to this was a shock to the system. I felt like a Victorian lady with an attack of the vapours just at the very thought of the décor and trappings I had inherited: I broke out into a cold sweat and could easily have swooned.

Never mind! I knew what I was in for, and I'd made up my mind. There's a saying in the hotel world: location, location, location—and that's what this had. We christened the hotel Mollington Banastre Hotel, because of its history. Little Mollington—also known as Mollington Banastre—was a township in the parish of St. Mary on the Hill, which was later merged into Mollington proper. People thought it a strange name at first, and it took them some time to get their tongues around it, but once they had, they never seemed to forget it—which was a big asset.

I had wanted a hotel in its own grounds, and I wanted a beautiful house. However, to get all that at a reasonable price, I had to put up with the shabby inside. As I had no more money, this was going to have to take a little while and come out of profits. Hence the first thing I had to address was to dramatically change the way in which it was run, which seemed to have been rather like a club, run for the benefit of the members or casual visiting clients, regardless of how much it was costing.

So I gradually phased all this out, and started to get the sales mix more in accordance with what I thought it should be. Then I set about getting the service right, which I knew how to do; after all, I'd been training all these years. However, this was a small, unknown business and not the business I was used to, and the standards were, I have to say, poor.

So, Christmas arrived, and with it, Christmas Day in particular. To my sheer horror, Mr McFarlane had previously arranged three—not just two, but three!—sittings for Christmas Day lunch. By the time we came to the second sitting, we had nowhere for people to go, and people waiting for the third sitting were sitting crouched on the staircase waiting. I was mortified. Imagine that at the Georges V or Gleneagles! I really don't know how they put up with it, and I don't know how I got through Christmas as a whole! But time went on and Christmas passed without incident or complaint. In January, we had the ballroom full to capacity, which was no bad thing, and it ran very smoothly.

So we'd started a new year, and I began to find my feet, and take action on my New Year's resolutions to turn this place into a hotel worthy of my training and experience. My original thoughts were that this rag-tag and bobtail of staff really had to go in order for me to get anywhere close to the standards I aspired to and was used to. So, slowly but surely I managed to 'let them go', and changed each and every one of them.

Then I had the thorny area of the kitchen. The head chef, Reynolds, had been there for some considerable time under the previous owner, and he seemed to be quite satisfied with what was coming out of his kitchen. Now, for basic standards, I suppose it was all right; but it was highly erratic and volatile, depending on the mood he was in; or, should I say, depending on how much he had drunk.

So, this ended up, he flared up like mad, got hold of a chopper and chased me round and round the kitchen until I could get some access to . . . So as he was chasing me round, I managed to get out.

Reynolds, the head chef, lived in the staff quarters in the converted stable block of this 1848 Victorian building. There were five rooms for living-in staff, and the head chef was one of them. His room was absolutely dreadful! He apparently just stepped out of the clothes he'd worn, and left wrinkled heaps of them around the floor. Every surface, including the carpet, was scattered with empty beer bottles, newspapers, dirty crockery and overflowing ashtrays. The stale smell hit you as soon as you opened the door. I can't comprehend how such a person could actually live like that! He ran the kitchen by screaming and shouting at people, and drank far too much, especially on Saturday nights. Invariably, he just staggered into bed, drunk, then fell unconscious until he groggily awoke the next day, and you never knew what was going to happen.

It all came to a head one Saturday night. We were well known for steaks, but instead of cooking each steak to order, he'd cut one big joint off the whole rump, slap it on the stove to cook, then just cut it into three and send it out like that. Well, this sort of carry on was really getting me down, so in the end I had to go and tell him off.

So I thought, "Well, if we don't get this right, I'm going to get nothing right," and I started to tackle him on the problems, saying I wasn't happy with the standard of service, the quality of food, the standard of hygiene, and above all, his understanding of the gross profits.

"Look here, Reynolds," I said, "This standard really isn't what I'm looking for."

He frowned at me through his bushy eyebrows, his fleshy lips almost forming a sneer. His red-rimmed eyes seemed to waver blankly, as if struggling to focus.

I seethed, "And this drunkenness is totally unacceptable!"

With an uncharacteristic burst of energy, and a mighty roar, Reynolds lurched his sweating carcass to his feet, grabbed hold of the kitchen chopper, and chased me round the kitchen, really intent on harming me.

Releasing a cacophony of swear-words and animalistic grunts, he lumbered after me as I took to my heels, racing around the counter until in the end I dived out of the kitchen and sprinted away. I went to my office and had a coffee to calm down, my shaking hands rattling the cup and saucer like castanets. Unsurprisingly, the next morning I told him to pack his bags and go. He could hardly protest!

Luckily, this was still January and the hotel was relatively quiet. I had no alternative but to get out my kitchen whites, go into the kitchen and take command myself. I suppose this was the making of the hotel and the beginning of our success, because I started to put into practice what I'd been taught by all those famous people in the hotel industry.

"There will be no more swearing tolerated anywhere in the kitchens or the rest of the hotel," I said sternly, eyeing that motley crew. "Let me make it perfectly clear. From this day forward, anyone found disobeying this order will be asked to leave the premises."

It never happened at Gleneagles, and it wasn't going to happen in my hotel.

I began to make up my own menus, appointed my own staff, had the kitchen stripped out, totally cleaned and painted the hotel, and by the Spring I had recruited a fairly decent staff, hopefully loyal enough and able to run the kitchen for some time to come. So everybody knew the standards of food, service and cleanliness that I expected in the restaurant, the ballroom, the banqueting and the guest rooms.

I appointed Maisie Jones to manage the reception office. Alongside her, I appointed a retired lady called Phyllis Seddon part-time to do the book-keeping and the accounts, for what they were worth. Barbara Gill joined us to look after the bar, work in the restaurant, and all over the place. She was only just a slip of a young girl, but I liked her very much and she had a lot about her. This was in 1965, and Barbara Gill is still employed today in the hotel. In the restaurant, I managed to build up a team of Spanish and Italian waiters who added a bit more class in that room, because by nature the Spaniards and Italians have always been good at their jobs, and they certainly gave the restaurant some polish. Joan Comber, who lived in a small village 20 miles from Chester, joined as head housekeeper, and she lived in. So that was all that taken care of!

We went merrily along, and things were settling down, the only thing was that I had to find a new chef. I was making some sort of profit, and I was really happy to try and persuade somebody to come and join me, knowing that we were to make positive strides forward.

I found a brilliant head chef: a man in his 40s called Eric Warham, who lived in Southport with his wife and two young children—one daughter and one son. He didn't seem to mind working the week, and having Sunday and Monday off—which is what most of my heads of department did, because those were the quietest days. Eric was a character and a half! He was always so buoyant and friendly; he loved to come out of the kitchen into the restaurant to meet the customers he cooked for, and he'd go into the bar and talk amiably to people. It really enhanced people's experience to chat to someone so passionate about food, and their work. He was professional, approachable and highly skilled, so I was delighted that he'd joined us. His presence really began to set new standards.

At 40, he had had plenty of experience and he would stay with me for just over 12 years. But his leaving was not intentional at all. A sad loss all around.

Because of my background in kitchens, and the way he operated, we complemented each other extremely well and things at the hotel began to get better and better. The rapport between us was almost unbreakable, since he performed just as I'd asked him to. He was such a laugh! His great hobby was buying old cars, doing them up a bit and selling them on, to supplement his salary. He'd fill in all the bodywork damage with fibreglass, then spray-paint it and you wouldn't know the repair was there; except, of course, that it was. So in the afternoons on the split duty, you would often find him underneath a car, doing bodywork repairs. And I have to say, I totally disapproved, because he managed to get bits of tin can and aluminium and staple machines everywhere. Anyway, that kept him happy, until he unfortunately died of cancer.

But for the 12 years he was with me, he was nothing but great fun to work with and we got on like a house on fire. He really understood my style, my standards, and we were both so happy working together, that's why he stayed for so long. He never once raised a kitchen chopper to me, either. I eventually employed Eric's son and Eric started to train him. Later on, I managed to send his son up to Gleneagles, funnily enough, to carry on his training, for which he was forever grateful. But when Eric died, I thought it was unwise to bring a young boy down to do such a job at that age, so I found a gentleman by the name of Ron Knox who lived in the little village of Saughall, three miles from us. He was married to a teacher in a local school, and he had a young boy and a young girl. He was a far cry from Eric in personality: although Ron's quality in cooking was no doubt equal to Eric's, his understanding of figures was considerably better, and his control of the kitchen was slightly different. But you have to give the head of department his say, or don't employ him, as I well knew from my days in Scotland.

By the time I employed Eric, all we had to do was get somebody decent to run the restaurant, and Eric happened to know a young man living in the village who was willing to join the team because he'd heard how we were building it up. I also managed to get hold of a young assistant manager from Liverpool at the Stork Hotel. So with that, the team was more or less complete, and things began to improve.

Every ha'penny I had, I spent replacing old-fashioned furniture in those early days. You'll be as amazed as me that I managed to get a customer at all! But slowly things came on, and the year went by really to my satisfaction.

The next Christmas came and we were much more organised. Eric did some fabulous buffet work, which saved him cooking for every individual's meal. The whole experience of Christmas went down a bomb, really. One of the members of staff—usually me—always dressed up as Father Christmas and came into the hotel just before lunch, laden with presents we'd got for the children.

Now, slowly but surely, we were beginning to run the hotel on the footing I required. We had 12 nicely appointed bedrooms, and this hotel was set, I have to say, in the most spectacular gardens you can imagine. But with three full-time gardeners, I suppose that's what you would expect. Mr McFarlane seemed to have paid more attention to the grounds than to running the hotel. Anyway, that was his affair. I was a beneficiary, and I began to love them myself so much that I carried on paying as much attention to the gardens as the hotel for the rest of my time there.

Then, something happened that was to change my life, although I had no idea at the time.

Chapter 10

Arrival of my first love affair

Monsieur Bontot, who was my boss and very good friend at the Georges V, rang me in April saying that he had a French girl working for him who wanted to come to England to learn English. He sold her very well.

I said, "Well, Michel, on your recommendation, and only because of that, I'm prepared to take her. She can learn English and return to France whenever she wants."

So this young girl, Gabrielle Jallais, known as Gaby, arrived in May 1965. I decided to put her in the cocktail bar, because she was very attractive, and I had nowhere else I could put her really, because the reception office and accounts were fully occupied. Anyway, she wanted to learn English, so I thought she would muddle through. People would have a good laugh at her attempts to converse, which was no bad thing for customer entertainment, and hopefully things were going to work out.

I then promptly went on holiday with Lawrence to Egypt and spent three weeks going down the Nile. We met two Belgian girls, funnily enough, and spent the holiday with them, speaking French. I returned home at the beginning of June, and this young girl, Gaby, was really down in the dumps, because she was feeling lonely and homesick, was struggling a little to converse, and had nobody to speak to in French. Well, I was home now, so she could speak to me, and of course, that made her happier.

I would always greet her in French, and have a little conversation with her every time I saw her, and her eyes would light up.

By now, I had bought a little red MGB sports car. One day, I was driving into town and on my way, I spotted that Gaby was walking in that direction, too, so I stopped the car to give her a lift. We chatted, of course, as we often had, but I was not ignorant of her charms, and by now things were beginning to progress. That was the start of the forbidden sin of management going out with members of staff. So, sin happened. I continued to go out with Gaby, and she used to come up to my elegant flat—which was huge: the size of the ballroom really, because it was right above it. It had this most gorgeous sitting room overlooking these beautiful gardens, with two bedrooms and a kitchen. She often used to come upstairs, sometimes on her own and sometimes with me, till one day a member of staff came up, knocked on the door, and accidentally saw Gaby up in my flat. Well, it wasn't too long before the entire staff knew that I was going out with this young lady.

Maisie Jones in the reception office did her very best to keep it under the carpet, but once a rumour starts, you know what it's like!

From a tiny spark, a fire had started.

Of course, it was such a juicy piece of news that it wasn't at all long before the entire staff knew that I was going out with Gaby. But when it happened, everybody seemed to accept it, so it seemed to make no difference, really. The months went by and we had a happy summer, business was relatively good, and Gaby and I fell so much in love that we were inseparable. Her funny little French accent and her lovely ways, never mind her charm and good looks—they all bowled me over so much, that on Christmas Day 1965, at lunchtime, I asked her if she would marry me. I was very pleased to say that she said yes!

So, then we had some difficulty since Gaby was French, living in England temporarily on a work permit. Similar problems occurred as I'd had in France. Anyway, that didn't worry me as much as the dread of facing the prospective in-laws for the first time. I had to get over my nervousness of going over to meet Gaby's family; in particular Gaby's father, to ask for his daughter's hand in marriage, which we did in February 1966.

"Of course they will love you!" Gaby assured me, but I remained unconvinced.

My whole future seemed to rest on this moment: I was more anxious asking her father than I was proposing to Gaby!

Thank goodness he readily agreed, and the whole family was ecstatic that Gaby had found such a nice husband.

With that out of the way, we decided to get married in May 1966 and started to plan the wedding. We went back to England and got technically married at Chester Registry Office –for the required civil legalities, then went out to lunch with just my parents and close family and my best man. We had a fabulous lunch, and chose a wine called Chateau Calon Segur, which was exceedingly well known, and the most beautiful wine. I liked it so much that on my journey home I bought a whole case, and we drank one bottle a year on a special occasion. My brother-in-law was often with us when we drank this; he adored wines as much as we did.

So, the date came in May for us to get married properly in church in France—with my family, friends and my best man there. The majority of the guests were Gaby's French friends and her family. Instead of catching the passenger ferry along with Lawrence and my sports car to get to France, I was audacious enough to travel to Calais on the Queen Mary, which was Britain's most beautiful liner at the time. They hoisted the car in and out of the hold. We had a most splendid lunch, a tour of the liner as we cruised across the Channel, and then slowly set off to drive to Gaby's house in Brittany.

Once we'd got there, the next two or three days were taken up with the final arrangements: going to the town hall, seeing the priest at the church, and meeting some more of Gaby's family: a flurry of introductions, socializing and preparations.

Then the day came for us to get married. Lawrence acted as my best man and we dressed in tails, which the French were most surprised to see because nobody in France dressed in tails, and we looked so smart, that I think it rather took people by surprise. We got married in a very lovely church within walking distance of Gaby's house, which was on the banks of the river, in Quimper, Brittany.

From the church we went to Sainte-Anne la Palud, this gorgeous restaurant on the edge of the beach. Gaby's elder brother and father arranged the wedding affairs at the restaurant, and we had the most fabulous leisurely lunch that lasted for hours and hours. The starters were live lobsters cooked fresh and served with three separate sauces, which were out of this world. I tried to persuade the chef to give me the recipe and he flatly refused. The odd times we went back to the restaurant in the following years, I always implored him to give me the recipe, but there was no way he was going to release his secret. I tried to recreate the sauces back home with Eric, my head chef, but even with all my knowledge of working with one of the most famous fish chefs from Gleneagles, I still failed, and I've failed up to today. So, there you go.

It seemed to be customary to these Bretons to get up and sing at the end of each course, and they expected our English contingent to do the same. Initially, as you might imagine, we were somewhat reticent and shy of sharing our talents, but never mind—with some nice wine, it soon all went down very well, as such things do at a wedding. So I can tell you, it was quite a pantomime, with Gaby's family singing ballads and sea-shanties in French and my family singing hymns and music hall ditties in English. Not quite a hip-hop rap battle, but competitive enough in a good-humoured way. It was most enjoyable, and never to be forgotten.

We set off on honeymoon to Lake Garda in Italy, and were driving down the Autobahn in Germany when I was distracted by a duck-egg blue blouse waving insistently at me through the rear window, rapidly followed by a blue skirt, white bra, and a fluttering of knickers flying in and out of view.

"Ahhhh! John!" Gaby squealed. "Stop! Stop!"

Through my rear-view mirror I could see all Gaby's honeymoon clothes sailing in the air down the motorway, to the bride's horror. Gaby's suitcase, strapped to the boot of my MGB on a proper rack, had somehow or other opened and shed its load. Anyway, we pulled up on the hard shoulder and sprinted madly back, dodging between lorries and cars, bending down and collecting her escaped clothing item by item, and eventually managed to get most of them back after some considerable time and mortal danger. We repacked and made our way for Lake Garda and our honeymoon, returning to England some three weeks later.

To sustain the celebratory occasion further still, I surprised Gaby with a trip back to England not on the ferry, as she'd expected, but on the Queen Elizabeth this time, a later liner than the Queen Mary, and we had our final gastronomic lunch on the ship before driving back home. On our arrival, all the entire staff were outside smiling, waiting to greet us.

We soon settled down to married life, living in this lovely flat and trying to give Mollington Bannastre some semblance of decency as a hotel. As I mentioned, we had already put some of the heads of departments in place and changed a lot of things. Whatever I'd done, I must have done right, as the hotel began to prosper.

Gaby kept complaining that her back was hurting, so we decided to take the step of going down to Gobowen, the most famous orthopaedic hospital in England. We saw Sir Reginald Watson-Jones, the senior orthopaedic consultant, whose father ironically had performed an operation on my mother; and he diagnosed that Gaby had damaged the three bottom vertebrae of her spine, undoubtedly due to her favoured sport of long-jumping when she was in France. He advised that Gaby really needed an operation to fuse these three vertebrae, which would then remove the pain. So, in the end we plucked up the courage and Gaby had the operation. In those days, these things did not repair themselves in a hurry. So, not only was I looking after the hotel, I was looking after my dear new wife, who then spent the next couple of months or so in bed at home, only very gradually getting up and back to normal.

One of the biggest highlights of the early life of the hotel was the 1966 FA World Cup. We magically managed to get the Bulgarian national team staying with us for three weeks. Funnily enough, they actually did quite well, and there was an enormous amount of excitement because they played about four or five matches and became quite serious contenders. We watched them training on the lawn of the hotel every day, except of course on the days that they were playing matches.

And then one day, the interpreter, who was their coach—a Frenchman—came and said, "We've asked the Brazilian team if they can come over and join us for a meal. Would it be possible?"

What? Well, I was jumping up and down! Pele, the world famous footballer, coming to dinner? I couldn't believe my ears!

In fact, by the time they'd finished inviting people, the party was growing and growing until it grew to over 100, which was no bother, because we had plenty of space in the ballroom, so 100 of them sat down to dinner—one of the greatest teams in the world, and one tiny little Bulgarian team, but the camaraderie was fantastic. In between each course the Brazilian team all sang a song; and of course, this got quite rowdy because the Bulgarians did the same. Our poor staff found it a hard job serving the different courses, because they were there, standing up swaying, singing away, in between courses, which we had not been prepared for, with us trying to get them to sit down again to serve the next course. It was quite a feat. Anyway, the evening ended successfully and the coach picked up the Brazilian team to take them to the hotel they were staying at.

Well, of course, finally, as we all well know, England won the cup. It was a very exciting period of our lives, in the hotel's infancy. And of course, our credibility shot up, out of all proportion—hosting a team was an enormous credit to us.

The birth of Interchange

The rest of '66 continued at a less hectic pace. We just got on with life and ran the hotel, but as I pored over the books, I began to feel that my knowledge of accountancy was a bit below par for running my own business, so I looked around to see what was available to help me. I came across a course on common hotel accountancy at Cornell University in the States, and thought, "Well, this is the one for me."

So, 1967 was the year I went to America, to Cornell University, to do an academic course in one of the finest universities in the world, which surprised everybody, but there you go. I went off to America to gain some more high-powered knowledge of accountancy and what one needs to look out for in running a hotel. And I have to say, the course was very good.

However, when I got home I kept saying to Gaby and the girls who looked after the accounts, "Really, what's the good of me being such a good accountant if one has no real business accounts to manage? We're only small."

I mean, we weren't turning over very much money.

I remember I met Leslie Richardson, who had the most beautiful hotel overlooking Torquay harbor, and I explained my worries to him.

"Do you know," I said, "I've got all this experience—years of training from working in some of the most famous hotels in the world . . . and I've just been on a high-powered course, that's made me even more enthusiastic to use my skills. But we just haven't got enough business. It's frustrating!"

And he seemed to be of the same view. So he said, "Well, let's do something about it. What we need is some package holidays to sell directly to the general public."

With that in mind, we decided we would split up the country: he would take the south and I would take the north, and we would recruit like-minded, good, privately-owned hotels into our venture. We managed to get twelve interested. We met in Bayswater in London for our inaugural meeting, and decided to move forward—this idea was, indeed, what we all wanted.

We named ourselves Interchange Hotels, and this was the birth of what was to become the largest and most powerful consortium of hotels in the world. But this, of course, took time, and you'll have to wait until later on for the full story.

We went about recruiting more members, with some success. It slowly grew, and we managed to persuade the hotelier in Bayswater to allow us to have part of the front hall for our own stand and a make-do office. To manage things, we even commandeered Bill Richards from the British Tourist Authority, who were most generous and supportive of our efforts for the next decade. So, there we were—Bill was installed in this office, no matter how modest and makeshift.

Back at my hotel, business continued and, luckily for us, it became highly profitable. I must have been doing something right!

Gaby got better, so we were very grateful for the operation. One piece of advice we were given was it really wouldn't be wise to have children because of the strain of carrying a child on Gaby's back. So of course, Gaby promptly became pregnant. In November 1967 our first daughter was born, whom we named Angelique. I was reading a French novel called *Angelique* and the title character was from the French aristocracy, so that's why I think I wanted to call her Angelique. On Christmas Eve, 1968, our second daughter was born, and we named her Christine. Gaby was in hospital under a private gynaecologist who rang me at lunchtime, with the hotel at its maximum capacity, and the restaurant bustling and crowded with everybody having their works' Christmas lunches. Things were really crazy, I was run off my feet, and I get this phone call from the gynaecologist saying, "Your wife is struggling in labour, Mr Mawdsley. We need to perform a Caesarean operation. Can we have your permission?"

I'll never forget it. Exasperated, I barked, "For goodness sake! You're the gynaecologist! Do what you think best—and get a move on, because I've got a busy restaurant to run!"

And I put the phone down. Some while later, I got another phone call saying that Christine was born safely and Gaby was all right. But neither of us will ever forget the laughter we've had from me telling the gynaeologist to "just get on with it!"

We then took the advice not to have any more children, so we were very happy with two nice young daughters. They were enamoured by the workings of the hotel; always playing in and around the housekeeping department. They became the apple of so many members of staff's eyes, it was incredible. So of course, that helped a lot, for both of us, as we had so many people wanting to look after them, acting as babysitters or nannies as they were growing up.

Because I was working morning and evenings, my work pattern gave me part of the afternoon off, so, I managed to be able to play with them all those years, which was quite rare—for a father to be able to have his children every day. Because of my own childhood, I was determined to make our family a proper family, and I made every endeavour to achieve that objective, which luckily I did, still to this day.

When the children were beginning to grow up we were living in the hotel, but should anything go wrong with the business, we would be homeless; which was a slightly dangerous proposition, from Gaby's and my point of view. So we bought a beautiful old farmhouse two miles from Corwen, up on the side of a mountain that overlooked the whole region towards Bala. You'd laugh, really, and we certainly laughed—because whilst we wanted a home, we didn't have that much money. We ended up by buying this house from the person who lived in it for under £2,000, but we hadn't even got all of that, so he lent us a private mortgage which we eventually paid off.

The farmhouse had two bedrooms and a bathroom upstairs; downstairs was a lounge, dining room and kitchen. The lounge was the most beautiful room, with oak-beamed ceilings, and we installed a proper solid fuel fire, as it had no central heating whatsoever. We eventually managed to buy some storage heaters, and then, at least, we started to get some warmth in the winter. Although it had a mile of its own private drive, which we had to maintain, and was very basic, it just seemed like heaven. We had no proper toilet facilities and no water, so we used to have to go up to the well every day to collect the water we needed for the house. Eventually I tired of this, and we installed a water supply and a proper septic tank. Somehow it was different from working on the hotel; we didn't mind working on it at all. And over the years, we did just that. We slowly renovated the house until it became quite beautiful and comfortable, and we adored just driving down there in our MG sports car.

The children gradually grew up and we sent them to Holywell St Winifred's Catholic School, a private school, as we didn't like the one in Chester. Angelique stayed there until she entered college to do her degree; Christine came home to Chester and went to high school to study for her A-levels.

With regard to Interchange Hotels, next, I was voted as Chairman of the company, and we successfully put together some holiday programmes for the tourist trade. And it took off quite remarkably. We began to grow more and more, needing bigger offices, and managed to find some in Richmond. Then Bill Richards returned to the British Tourist Authority so we looked for a new Chief Executive/Marketing Director, finding a guy called Tony Rothwell, who ironically joined us from Forte Hotels. Tony stayed with us for years and years until he emigrated to the United States.

So, we were now stabilised, we had a very good marketing director, and we were financially sound. We thrived, and I enjoyed being the Chairman. I went around the country visiting each member hotel, and was, of course, welcomed with open arms by the owners, getting to know each and every one very well.

The next major objective of the organisation, prompted by me, really, was a sort of coaching and mentoring provision. When you are a single hotelier with your own business, there's no head office to ask for help and no-one to turn to, so we decided that part of the remit of Interchange Hotels was for owners to help each other. So, if one had a problem, say, with them losing money on their food, others would come to his aid to see what he was doing wrong and offer support to put it right. This was an enormous benefit to independent hotel owners, because we'd never had this help before.

We continued with what we were doing, which rolled us into 1969, and it all created a fair amount of work—hotel, college, Interchange Hotels.

New developments

Our hotel was doing very well. The Government had issued a White Paper on tourism stating the insufficient number of high quality hotels in England, so they were going to offer an incentive to encourage the growth of more good hotels. They offered £1,000 per room built, so we took up the idea and raised the rest of the capital.

I started to design our first extension of 15 rooms and a conference room, and flew over to Copenhagen to the Trafalgar Hotel. I'd previously met the general manager and owners, who had built this brand new hotel in Copenhagen which had sounded fascinating. What intrigued me most was the bedroom construction. Instead of the plumbing being tangles of individual systems dotted about room to room, they had built the hotel rooms backing onto each other, with corridors between and central columns and service ducts running from floor to ceiling, which meant that you could get into these ducts to service the systems in any of the bedrooms without disturbing the clients. So I designed my hotel on that basis, and we were one of the first in England to do so.

You wouldn't believe the difficulty I had with the Planning Department to get this development through; the joining of the two buildings was a particular stumbling block. Anyway, Chester had appointed a gentleman to look after the interests of the city for the next ten years, to get some coordination in general planning applications, and he often stayed with me. I spoke to him about this problem, and he simply said, "Oh well, we'll soon sort that out."

He got a piece of paper and sketched a pergola linking one building with the next, and lo and behold, the planning authorities accepted it. Isn't it crazy? After all the months of anguish I'd had, I ended up erecting a cheap garden pergola to please them. It just shows you the bureaucratic nature of some of England's systems.

So now the expansion of the hotel from 12 rooms, to 15 more and another two conference rooms, was more than doubling the size we could cater for. Suddenly we had to upgrade everything, because we had only been a little hotel and now we were getting on to being a fairly substantial medium-sized hotel, with a fair amount of conference facilities, because we'd already inherited a big ballroom and now we'd added two more spaces: one to accommodate around 70 people, and another for up to 80 people. So now we had three conference rooms, which were big for business, especially for companies wanting a hotel in the calm of the countryside, yet near industrial centres and other companies. If you don't know it, Chester is really the jewel in the crown of tourism because of its historic Roman background, and is famous for its tiered shops. The whole of Chester is nothing but tourism, yet surrounding us was an enormous amount of industry and commerce in Warrington, Widnes and Runcorn, where there were big oil refineries. And of course Liverpool. So we had a vast catchment area in which to capture conference business. And I was right—we didn't fail in getting that at all.

We used a local builder, Bernard West, up the road, who seemed to do all our work for years and years afterwards. So now I felt that we were beginning to develop a real hotel. In 1970, the hotel was built, heralded by a lot of publicity. With close on 30 rooms, we were in a position to enlarge our market, and I progressed into business ventures with some coach operators, which I thought would have been a good, profitable way of helping to fill the rooms; I knew I'd got the business, and they knew that their accommodation was secure. So, this gave us guaranteed business every day of the week if we so desired, and occupied about 15 rooms, because each coach normally carried around 30 passengers. This continued for the next few years.

We weren't to know that one of the most alarming economically turbulent times was about to fall upon us. Inflation grew out of control and increased year by year until it reached just over 20 percent per annum. Well, can you imagine coping with a one percent inflation increase—every single month? It meant that we could no longer keep prices static at all, because they had to go up every few weeks, otherwise we would not survive. This nearly brought me down, because the coach companies I'd done business with wanted guaranteed prices a year ahead so that they could publish their holiday prices in their brochures. Well, as the months went by, with us being unable to raise prices to keep up with the cost of living, by the following year I found myself losing money. This went on for three years, and the government couldn't even get it under control. I decided I was no longer going to do business in this manner. I stopped dealing with coach companies and reverted to offering rooms only to private customers. It changed our market mix quite dramatically, as you could imagine, and I had to go searching for more individual clients. But never mind—we did so, and all went well, and I managed to get back into profit.

I was always looking for something new to offer clients, and a project to develop to maximize our business. We had a building at the end of the car park, which had been the stables, with a beautiful archway through to the courtyard at the back, which used to house two carriages and the horses for the owners of the house at the time. This was lying empty, and I decided, in my wisdom, that it could well be earning us money without us having to build anything more. So we decided to convert this beautiful coach house and stables into a pub.

Before it opened, I spent the next couple of years in some enjoyable research on pubs and on discovering the history of the local area.

I found that there had been a coach and four service from Chester to Liverpool via Eastham, leaving three times a week. From Chester it came up to our house, which was well known then as The Causeway, because the River Mersey and the River Dee used to flood across the causeway. This naturally became a tremendous hazard to the coach and four, which was called The Good Intent. Highwaymen were known to often hold up the coach to rob the passengers of their jewellery. On other occasions, the coach came to the house and swapped horses to carry on the journey. All of this was recorded in the documentation of the time. I enjoyed hunting down appropriate photographs and knick-knacks to suggest the theme, so we decorated the pub accordingly and called it The Good Intent.

We managed to get a young man from the local village, Alan Leicester, to become the manager and opened this pub with as much fanfare as possible, to let people know that the pub was now fully open and welcoming clients. We hired a coach and six, and Gaby, me and others all dressed in Victorian costume to ride on it. The carriage left Eastgate outside the Grosvenor Hotel in Chester to travel to The Good Intent, arriving at the pub for the official opening. Always open to a photo opportunity, we attracted a good deal of publicity. This venture was also greatly welcome in the local village because they had no pub, so it was an instant success. It also became the headquarters of Mollington Cricket Club, which was another new venture.

Since I was always trying to help young people to follow in my footsteps, I got involved with the college of further education, especially the catering department, and stayed with them for the next 22 years, ending up as the college's Vice-Chairman. So, over the years, I can tell you, this kept me rather busy on top of my other interests.

The American influence

Interchange Hotels had now grown to a membership of over 100 hotels. We met a gentleman who owned the L'Aigle Noir Hotel in Fontainbleau and was chairman of a French hotel organisation like ours, which offered us very interesting possibilities for alliance. And over the next few months, we gradually came across one or two smaller like-minded organisations in other countries, so we decided to meet up in Amsterdam to discuss the potential of working together.

David Baird-Murray, who owned a very large, beautiful busy conference hotel in Llandrindod Wells in Wales was Chairman of Interchange by now. He was also Lord Lieutenant of Mid-Wales, which entailed him doing a lot of diplomatic work. We all remember that in Amsterdam he kept saying that while he was there, he wanted to buy a diamond for his wife. Well, Gaby and I went along with him, and he did indeed buy his wife a diamond—to our utmost surprise, and perhaps some horror, since he paid £3,000 for it, which was a lot of money back in those days. So, his wife was going to get a lovely present!

One evening, we decided to take a stroll round Amsterdam and look at the girls posing in the windows, for which Amsterdam was famous. On our walk, we went into a bar to have some drinks and David started chatting to an American guy. It transpired that he was from a prestigious family in San Francisco, and was chairman of an organisation called Best Western Hotels, who had exactly the same ideas as we had in Europe. They might have had slightly different objectives, but then, that was their own purpose and direction. However, all the hotels were all privately owned and all were seeking to increase their business in a similar way to ourselves. So we said, "Why don't we get to know each other a little more, and maybe we can foster some cross-Atlantic business?"

And this partnership continued for the next several years. Our relationships with America and Europe grew. Our board went over to the States to their conferences, and learnt a great deal. Now, here in Europe, you think of a conference as a pretty formal affair, with lots of people sitting down in an auditorium, where a chairman opens the meeting and the conference commences. Not so in America, especially with Best Western. They would have the most fabulous theatrical starts to their conferences, and each year they aimed to outdo the last. One year we went over, they'd actually persuaded Disneyland to close for the first time in its history in order to host the Best Western convention there; so you can tell how well-respected their organisation was—and creative.

When we got home, this fantastical approach stayed in the back of our minds for a while and kept nagging at our board members, particularly Tony Rothwell, our Chief Executive; Mick and Jean Webb who were fairly flamboyant hoteliers who owned Moor Hall in Sutton Coldfield in Birmingham, and myself. It made quite an impression on us.

"Interchange Hotels needs to promote its name with the general public and the trade," we all agreed.

We created a marketing committee of about 10 hoteliers from around the country, with me as Chairman and Jean Webb as my Vice-Chairman. We started what we called workshops, hiring large rooms in London and capital cities around the world, and we would persuade each hotelier to have a cubicle of their own to promote their establishment. Under the umbrella of Interchange Hotels, we would invite the travel trade in for one day, holding parties and entertainment for them in particular, and on other days we would be open to the general public, launching Holidays to Great Britain, this highly successful motoring programme we had, going around Britain.

We met a guy called Patrick Henry, who was head of American Airlines' marketing department for inbound traffic. He immediately jumped on the idea of our motoring programmes and wanted to feature them in his inbound holiday brochure—which he did, with great success. This also formed the start of a great friendship between his wife and Gaby, particularly later on, when I became the Chairman of Interchange Hotels yet again.

These workshops became fairly flamboyant, especially when we were abroad. There was always fierce competition, especially to get hold of the travel trade, because they got fed-up of foreign people banging on their door wanting business. So instead of having the usual cocktail party reception or dinner party, we decided on the most novel idea of offering them a full English afternoon tea, as one would serve in England, with proper teapots, toasted teacakes and dainty little sandwiches. We organised this with one of the most famous hotels in Toronto, and just before tea was served, Mick and Jean Webb and I would come into the room to announce it. All very genteel and proper, except that we were dressed in underpants displaying the English national flag. Well, the press went crazy for this, and all the photographic coverage we received in the Toronto newspapers showed us that we had really done some terrific marketing. Business then poured in from the wholesalers for years to come; because of course, once you'd made contact with these people, you didn't let them go.

So, coming back to our experience at the annual conference of Best Western, this American style of presentation kept nagging at us, and wouldn't leave us alone. Our own conference was held in David Baird-Murray's hotel in Llandrindod Wells. We were very secretive about our plans, because we wanted to make a real impression on our fellow Britons, after the startling experience we'd had in the States.

The main ballroom was tightly guarded from the rest of the hoteliers, with the stage blacked out. The conference commenced with people being shown to their seats by ushers with torches in the pitch darkness. When everybody was seated comfortably, in total wonderment and anticipation, suddenly in the background one could hear the distant sound of a helicopter. This rotary blade 'ricka-ricka-ricka-ricka' noise got louder and louder, until a replica helicopter landed on the stage, which was illuminated to display a military operation, accompanied by troops of armed commandos, fully camouflaged.

"Everybody stay right where you are!" their commander-in-chief (in reality, the gentleman who was the voice of Darth Vader from Star Wars) announced. "I have come to take control of everybody in the hotel!"

Their rifles and machine guns swept the audience, who sat, dumbstruck, unable to believe their eyes. There was general amazement, amusement or horror that we'd had the audacity to start an annual conference for hoteliers in this frivolous way. But it certainly made a lasting impression!

We continued the theme throughout the next three days, with these commandos suddenly appearing at lunch, or during cocktail parties, and taking people hostage. They made it great fun. It did give the conference a much more lighthearted start and certainly gave people something to talk about, far more than any other conference anyone had attended. Of course, everybody was keen to find out what the theme would be the next time. The next year's was based on Sherlock Holmes, with the same gentleman taking the title role. This kind of spectacle became the format of the conference for years, and really did help to encourage the members to attend.

Throughout this period, about 20 or 30 hoteliers went over to America on frequent visits, to try and improve the rapport and relationship between America and Europe, and always went to the

American convention. In the process, of course, you made personal friends and we would often stay at one of the American hotelier's hotels or their home, which was great fun, especially for those of us who went every year. And in time, our chairman was invited to some of their board meetings. So, this became a combination of serious business and light relief from the everyday grind of running the business.

The arrival of my first horse

Back home, I was working too hard. My doctor was seriously concerned for my health, and told Gaby that something must change. I needed to slow down, or get a hobby or get out, because the workload of the hotel, Interchange Hotels, and the college was beginning to get on top of me.

"You're going to be seriously ill if you don't do something," he warned, staring at me from beneath furrowed brows. "Find a hobby!"

A hobby? I knew how to play golf very well but that didn't tempt me.

Well, one New Year's Eve, a group of us were at the bar, well after midnight, and I was buying a round of drinks. One of our local farmers, Ted, was relaying the story that his daughter had a horse and was beginning to get a bit tired of it—boys seemed to be the bigger attraction, so the poor horse never got much of a ride these days.

"So if you fancy taking up riding, John . . ." he grinned.

My mind suddenly sprang to the thought that I was looking for a hobby. "Do you know—I just might!" I said.

"Great!" he grinned, and raised his glass of whiskey. "Would you like to come over to the farm then, and give it a ride? Come round in the morning and we'll go out."

So, when the morning came, I was still sober enough, so I decided to take him up on this offer. So, lo and behold, on New Year's Day, I went round to the farm where he was busy in the milking parlour. Through the steamy, milky atmosphere, he came out and smiled saying, "Right, you want to ride my daughter's horse. I'll go and get her," which he promptly did.

Jessie came downstairs quite cheerily, and said, "Hi! Dad told me you were going to ride Flossy, so we'll go and get her."

So, off we go to the stable, and this beautiful grey—in fact, more or less white—mare, about 12 years old, was brought out. And I got on this lovely, soft grey mare with some trepidation, having not ridden a horse before in my life. I was led out to the fields and just told to 'ride her', which I did, gently walking around the farm for about an hour, and I found, to my surprise, that I thoroughly enjoyed it.

When I got back to the farmhouse, both Ted and Jessie came out to see me, grinning, and asked, "How did you get on?"

"Oh," I said, unable to hide my delight, "I loved it!"

"Well, why don't you come tomorrow, too?" laughed Jessie. "Go out and ride her, because she's not been ridden for ages."

So I promptly did. I somehow got the bug for riding.

And eventually, over the next few months, I got to know the horse very well. I really fell for this new hobby. Jess was about 18 and really more interested in boys and cars than horses, and of course, it didn't take long for me to fall in love with Flossy, and I ended up buying her. I had a lot of outbuildings at home and a paddock, so I brought the horse home and I carried on riding, and quite often took it down to the farmhouse with us, where I also had a small, enclosed paddock.

One day when the horse was there, I met Lord Newborough, the owner of the estate from whom we'd bought our house, and we got chatting. I got to know him quite well over the years, and he seemed to like us—although he didn't like the Welsh too much! He commented on the horse and asked, "Well, where do you go riding? What do you do with her?"

I said, "Well, I go wherever I can."

And all of a sudden, he just said, "Well, as far as the eye can see, most of this land is mine. You can ride wherever you like. And in the forests there are trails galore, so go out and enjoy yourself."

So of course, I did. And then I fell more and more in love with riding. I'd both fulfilled the doctor's recommendations and found a hobby I liked.

Mollington was a small community, and if you ever went into our pub at about seven o'clock, you'd meet everyone. One evening, I met a guy called Harry Kay, a finance director to a big company that made components for the brewing industry, who had the most beautiful house in Mollington. They had horses, and he invited us over to ride together. His daughter, Judith, was most adventurous: she'd get us out and doing more things. I then joined a riding club and started to ride even more, and even learned to jump.

Harry Kay had a friend, another farmer up on the Wirral, Fred Lancaster. Fred adored riding and hunting, and had a big farm with acres of woodland, which he had developed into his own cross-country course. I was invited to go riding with him one Sunday morning, and Harry said, "Well, we'll meet at Fred's house and then go on from there."

Now, I arrived there just after Harry, not realising that at eleven o'clock, Bess, Fred's wife, brought out a salver of silver chalices filled with sherry, which we drank before setting off to ride into this large woodland. And of course, we were like children riding round this wood, grinning with glee, thundering between the shady trees, coming across hedges and jumping jumps which we didn't expect. This was Fred's pastime, making secret jumps to surprise us. We'd have great fun playing with our horses until it was time to go home for lunch. And this became a regular occurrence, for years and years to come.

The following winter, Fred said, "Would you like to go hunting?" which took me by surprise. He said, "I go every week. You can go with me."

So he introduced me to Philip Hunter, who was the Master of Cheshire Forest Hunt, who invited me to join as a member, and I promptly accepted. Just for a trial, I took my white horse, Flossy, hunting near Fred's in the Wirral in case something went wrong and I wanted to come home. Flossy wasn't really too enamoured with this, since she hadn't done it before and wasn't particularly good at going or jumping freely, so it made me a little nervous. However, I carried on anyway for the whole of the season, met a lot of new friends and thoroughly enjoyed myself.

The following season I said, "Well, if I'm going to go hunting, I think I'll go and buy a proper hunter," so my next job was to go searching for a horse. I bought a nice Bay, but it had some odd quirks— he didn't really like jumping straight at the jump. In fact, the only way I could get him to jump was to run along the hedgerow and turn suddenly, and then he would jump immediately. You would have to twist and go, jumping sideways and almost coming out of the saddle. To everybody's amusement!

I couldn't stand that any longer, so the following year, I bought a big Bay horse from the South Notts hunt—a really lovely animal. But he'd come from a hunt where they jumped stone walls all the time and he hadn't even seen a hedge before, so he shied away from them and did not want to jump a hedge to save his life!

Barbara, another farmer in Mollington who hunted with the Cheshires, said, "Well, come round to the farm with him. We'll get you boxed in, I'll have the whip at the back of you, and after a few tries, hopefully we'll get the horse to jump."

Well, it took ages and ages, but we persevered because the horse was so lovely. Anyway, in the end, Barbara managed to get him to go over, and I was so thrilled! Barbara was laughing her socks off that we'd finally achieved it.

So, now I was equipped with a very fine, dark Bay hunter, who would go anywhere in the end. So that was me all set for the hunt— fully fledged, fully hooked, and there was no way I would ever miss a

Wednesday. I couldn't go out on Saturdays because the hotel was too busy, but on Wednesdays I could take the day off. It was our own business and doing well, so I could afford to take a day out every week. I made a lot of friends, in particular a doctor from a bit further up the Wirral, John Prest. I used to go out for the day, taking a sandwich with me prepared by the hotel kitchen, and I bought a hipflask which I always kept replenished with decent sloe gin. And slowly I became very popular with a great many friends!

We bought a little grey pony called Spray for the children when they were 10 or 12, and they were enticed—or they pestered me, rather—to come hunting. The first year, I used to take the girls out hunting on the leading rein, and they were really excited and enthusiastic. Indeed, we all had this passion for hunting that's stayed with us right through my life. Fox hunting was quite legal in those days; it was a sport and whether you supported it or not was up to your own conscience. We liked it and we carried on hunting right through to the ban. And in actual fact, the girls are still hunting today. The children were at school on weekdays, so we had to go out on a Saturday.

So there we were, the whole family, hunting every week. And since I was now going on both Saturdays and Wednesdays, I decided that I would buy another horse. A guy called Marcus—or Mark—Chambers, who was a horse dealer, hunted with the Forest. His son, who was about 20, was the whip who rode up front with the hounds on a fine black horse that seemed to go everywhere. I pestered and pestered Mark for this horse.

He said, "No, it's my son's. You can't have it."

Well, I didn't give up, and eventually must have worn him down. One Christmas Eve, as he was coming in home, I said again, "Marcus, you know, I really want to buy the horse."

He trotted along beside me, his lips shut tight and squinted hard at me, as if weighing me up for one final time. Eventually, he grinned and said, "Yeah, I think you'd be well suited to it."

So Mark, in the end, gave in and I bought this lovely black horse I'd longed for.

We now had three horses in the stables. Time progressed, and the following season the children didn't want poor little Spray anymore—they wanted a decent hunter.

I asked Mark, "Can you find me a decent horse for the children?"

Well, funnily enough, the previous season the huntsman had had an accident and shot his hand, and needed a horse that was calm so he could ride one-handed, and this horse was called Gunner. Well, when his hand recovered, he wanted to revert back to a more fiery animal to take him properly up front with the hounds, and I was offered Gunner. We had it for quite a while without paying anything. Well, the children fell in love with this horse, and no way was it going to go back. In fact, it stayed with us for the next dozen years. The children grew up and hunted it as young ladies, when they got their proper dress, looking so smart. The whole Mawdsley family turned out, and sometimes I would turn out with two horses myself so that I could change halfway, because I liked to ride up front and would really go. I got the bit between my teeth and I liked to be as near as the front as I could possibly get, riding hard. So, no matter what obstacle came before us, I needed a horse that was capable of taking five foot hedges. So I'd take both of them—Milton, my black horse, and Beady, the big Bay.

One day I was on Milton, up front with Ron, the huntsman, going through a farmyard. We were racing downhill on the drive for the cattle, with the hounds screaming their heads off, and I was flying. We saw a gate ahead. Well, we were in such a hurry that Ron said, "No way can we stop and fiddle with opening the gate! We'll have to jump."

I saw him do it, so I just flew over with no trouble whatsoever—except on the opposite side was the farmyard with all the cow muck mess. My horse slipped and skidded on landing, and still holding the reins, I fell, sliding headfirst, down into the slurry pit, sinking to below my head. The horse then followed me, so we were both in the slurry pit, completely covered in greeny black cow muck and God knows what.

Well, this of course, caused enormous laughter amongst everyone, and lots of people stopped in their tracks, doubled over with guffaws. To hell with the hunt—this was hilarious entertainment!

One good friend I used to hunt up front with, David Whelan, who owned JJB Sports, the big company for sports clothing and equipment, kindly got me out of the slurry pit. We got the horse out, and then commandeered the big farm hosepipe, double the size of a normal one, with enormous pressure because it was used to hose the farmyard down. He put me against the wall and blasted me to hose me down as best as he could. We then hosed the horse down, and I jumped back on and carried on hunting for the next hour. The speed we were going kept me warm, but later on things got a bit slower and I was getting cold.

So I said to Jane, Mark James's eldest daughter, who lived nearby, "Is there any way I can get changed?" So we promptly went to her house. Of course, I smelt like . . . I don't know what! Anyway, I went into the house, had a shower, and suddenly remembered that I had no clean clothes to put on.

"Oh, John," Jane laughed, "I only have my own clothes—but you're welcome to borrow something!"

"I'll be grateful for anything!" I smiled.

Being a very feminine girl—or else having a very wicked sense of humour—the only ladies' wear Jane had available was a pink, frilly, floral blouse and a pair of lilac jodhpurs. I had no choice. It was either those or unspeakable wet filth. I got dressed in her clothes, promptly returned and carried on, to the huge laughter of everybody yet again to see me dressed in Jane's clothes. The children, of course, were in fits, seeing my dilemma.

Eventually I'd had enough, so I put the horse away, went to the pub, and it was really quite funny. That was one of the most memorable days we could ever have had.

There were several people who became very close friends. One couple was David and Pam Webber who had the Peppertree Hotel in Santa Barbara, and they lived in a house called Hope Ranch. It was a bungalow, and the sheer size of it was awe-inspiring: there were seven bedrooms, acres of ground, stabling for six horses, all overlooking a bay in California. Staying there was sheer heaven, and the extra benefit was that Gaby always came with me. The attraction for me was that David and Pam were both passionate about riding and went hunting on Saturdays, just like we did.

On one of our visits, they suggested that next time I would go hunting with them, so of course I was over the moon. I was fascinated, too, and asked, "Well, what do you hunt?"

"Oh, we don't hunt like you in England," they said. "We hunt coyote and wild boar."

The terrain is quite mountainous and there are a lot of gorges, so you try to ride on the top of the ridges, while the hounds hunt down in the gorges. You have to be fairly agile, because a lot of the time you have to go up and down these ridges. But that didn't worry me in the least. If you've got a good horse, you're safe and sound.

So, the next visit we went, it was agreed that we were going hunting, so of course I took all my English hunting gear. Well, they were flabbergasted to see me turn out exquisitely dressed, in my red hunting coat, top hat and polished boots. They all turned out in ratcatchers: tweed coats and breeches, but they got used to me hunting in English hunting gear. We used to set off at six o'clock in the morning and as long as we finished by lunchtime, when it got too hot for me, I was fine. And we had tremendous fun. We would end up the day by having a big barbeque, all very informal. Americans are like that—you have to get used to them, because if you can't cope with them, you may as well give up. On the other hand, their hospitality is beyond anybody's I've ever come across. They always lent me their horse, Silver, and he was in fact silver-grey. And often, the hounds would corner a wild boar in the crevasse, and the huntsman would go down and shoot him and they would bring him home. And eventually, we would get joints of wild boar to eat. They'd also hunt these coyote that ran like fury, which was terrifying sometimes, because the speed at which everybody travelled to keep up with the hounds, without anything to jump or to slow you down, was the thrill of a lifetime.

They have a hunting week and I was invited to go over and stay with them for it. And it was most unusual, in that 25 of us would hunt for a week. We set off on the first day and drove about 25 miles up to Ronald Reagan's ranch which of course was beautiful, to say the least. We hunted normally from six o'clock to midday, and had our freedom to hunt where we wanted to. Sometimes we met the owners, sometimes we didn't. But the day finished at midday, when we'd have a barbeque, then we'd put up the horses and then we would drive about 25 miles from there to somebody else's ranch, where we would all stay. So there's 25 people, mostly in couples, and we'd stay at that ranch and have a dinner barbeque or party with them and their cowboys. All these people were cattle breeders and all had their own cowboys—so like the real world of the Wild West, if you like, because that's what it felt like to me. And when you had a steak, they just took a whole slice of rump and you had this enormous size of piece of meat, which I could no way think of eating. They couldn't understand that I ate so little. And the next day, we would do the same thing, and this went on for a week. It just became a lot of fun.

You got to know each other fairly well when you were riding. There was a single American girl my age who was very attractive and a lot of fun. I always rode with her somehow, and I think I'll say no more, there, really. The week finished, with us exhausted, muscles aching like mad for having ridden for six days in a row for six hours a day, and then it was time to go home.

On another occasion, Gaby came over because instead of staying with David and Pam, we were staying with Pete and Marie-Lou Worts, who had a typical American motel just out of Phoenix, in the countryside. A lot of the Americans had motels, and they had a lovely one which was very successful. They made a lot of money and enjoyed life a lot. He had a pet Harley-Davidson, which he used to love riding; a great friend who played polo, and this beautiful six-seater jet in his own hangar at the local airport. And he would take the car down, pull the plane out, and all he'd do was get in and go—as easy as that. They had a wooden-built ranch house up in the mountains, and when we went and stayed with them, they would often say, "Come on, let's spend the weekend up in the country."

Funnily enough, he was very close to John Wayne's estate, and Pete was friendly with the Wayne family, so we would often meet John Wayne either in the restaurant for dinner or at each other's houses, and it was great fun seeing this superstar. I've still got a little gold lighter which he had inscribed for me, and I treasure it, because we had so much fun in their company.

Then on another occasion, we were with David and Pam and they suggested that we had our holidays over there.

Service Is Our Specialty!

Chapter 15

Holidays

During the '70s we lived a relatively normal life. The children were growing up, we had a little Morris Minor for Gaby to do the school run to the bus, and the hotel grew from strength to strength. It was a while yet before I could get rid of these damned schoolroom chairs from the ballroom which I disliked intensely, but ironically our customers didn't seem to mind once the tables were all dressed up. We had our holidays in the South of France and took the children, and because we liked it so much in Cavaliere, we tended to go on holiday somewhere in the South of France almost forever more, bar one or two odd holidays to the Algarve or somewhere similar.

Pamela Davies-Webber from the Peppertree Inn at Santa Barbara in California suggested that we all went on holiday together. The four of us, four of them, and two friends; so we had a party of 10. We had chosen to go down the Colorado River. So with much excitement from all concerned, we chose the month of August to stay with them on the ranch for about three weeks or more, and chose to go on the long trip. We set off from the very start, rafting down the Colorado River. It was a journey that was going to take us 10 days before we came out to the end of the Colorado River's run, into Lake Tahoe. It was beautifully warm weather, the river was warm, when we set off with nearly half a day's preparation and training. We had three big, rubber rafts and a wider, long supply boat that followed us, bringing part of the crew and all the supplies we were going to need, and probably more than you could imagine, for ten whole days.

I don't like going underwater; in fact, I positively detest it. However, our training course meant that we had to do it, because our guides were very sure that when we came to the rapids it was very likely that the raft would topple over or one of us would fall out. So we had to know how to look after ourselves. It sounds very frightening at the beginning, but where we were, it was really calm and the river was quite small. I don't know whether you've ever seen Colorado in the desert, but its river starts off on ground level. As we proceeded over the next ten days, we would be 3,000 feet below ground level, so we were all strictly warned that if we wanted to continue with the holiday, that was the final decision. If we felt we wanted to leave, we must leave now, because there was no way we would get out of the river to ground level as normal except via helicopter. It would drop down to collect someone in an emergency, but that would be highly expensive.

So we all got in our gear and set off on this gentle run of the water on the three rubber rafts. Then we found there was another party of ten, mostly men, unconnected with us, who were travelling at about the same time. Funnily enough, we became very friendly with each other: so much so that we decided that we would stop and camp at the same place as them each night, and have more fun round the camp fires. You would think that ten days would be a long time confined to rafting, but it whizzed by. The scenery was beyond belief day by day as we gradually got lower and lower down the gorge through which the river runs, and the way in which it has eroded the sides over the thousands of years is phenomenal. You can see the striations quite clearly, the changing colours of the rock and the foliage, and the places where the Indians used to have their caves. And as we set off calmly, drifting really—I don't think we ever used the motor except in trouble, and we never seemed to paddle except to keep the raft in the right direction we were going. None of us were quite used to such peace and tranquility, because there was absolutely nobody else to be seen and all we could see were the sides of the mountains that climbed way above us.

The first night we stopped, we actually got a bit of a shock because it started to rain and we all had to erect our tents. I had not erected a tent since I was a boy scout, and I seemed to be getting the thing more or less upside down, to everybody's sheer amusement, especially my two daughters'. Anyway, we gradually got it right, since we did have to sleep under canvas that wet evening. However, for the rest of the journey we slept under the stars, and it really was such a beautiful experience to wake up in nature and wash in the river. I shaved with a tiny mirror on the side of the banks. Gaby and I, with our ailments, bangs and bruises from previous events in life, decided that we would take a blow-up double mattress, to everybody's amusement. However, it worked very well, so we had this lovely mattress to sleep on. We went to sleep as the sun went down, which was quite early, and we woke up with the sunrise and the stars still out, casting various beautiful lights on the bronze-coloured stone. We had real camp fires, where we'd set up tables and cook proper meals. We had a good fry-up for breakfast and a varied menu for dinner, and we'd got our drinks and wine, and plenty of beer. The guys from the other party seemed to like their beer. And as the sun died down, we had bonfires, so we all sat round the fire and had our dinner, and eventually it would end up in a sing-song and party, which was quite a novel experience.

As the week progressed the river narrowed, and as it narrowed the waters ran faster. After about three days of calm and tranquility, the river suddenly changed into an angry force of water, and it took quite a bit of work from our experienced guide to keep our raft on the straight and narrow on the racing river. To start with, nothing went wrong and we'd get through the rapids at enormous speed, bouncing up and down and holding on for dear life. And then we'd get a day of peace again, and our friendship, from being confined together, grew and grew.

Everybody got on with each other; we'd have water fights in the river and try and race each other sometimes, all in great fun. So now we were into our fifth or sixth day. As we progressed, the water became quite fierce, and we were warned that this was the time that we would be likely to either capsize the raft or one of us would fall off. In actual fact, he made us fall off so we could know what to expect. And as much as I dislike it, most of us managed it and got back on the raft easily enough.

I'd seen this water rafting on films and TV, but I didn't really realise how hair-raising it actually was. These rafts hurtle down the rapids at enormous speed, and one minute you were facing enormous boulders in the river, thinking, "Any minute now we're going to crash," but somehow the river, in its way, looked after us. Most of the time, with the guidance of our guide, we would keep flowing with the water. And of course, going down these rapids, we were going downhill at some almighty pace, and luckily enough, none of my family fell overboard, but a couple of the other guys did. Our supply boat, which was about half a day or more behind us, actually got stuck on some of the rocks. Eventually, we would pull in for lunch, which was really more of a snack than anything else, and some beer, then we would continue the journey down until the evening, when we would once again strike up camp and have our meals and sing-songs, never knowing the next day if we were going to have a more peaceful day or if the rapids were going to get stronger than ever. And at times they did, and it became quite frightening.

The supply boat eventually managed to get off the rocks it got caught on. Luckily enough, we were all right. But about three quarters of the way through the journey we learned that on the previous run down, one of the boats got stuck and someone had unfortunately died, which of course frightened us a little. However, we continued this exotic, exciting journey until the river flowed gently into this lovely lake, with the water all brown, after being churned up from coming down the rapids. And gradually, we put the motor on and drove across the lake into pure, beautiful, silky water, where we all washed and shampooed ourselves, after having felt quite dirty.

And sadly, the holiday was over. For all of us, I think it remains one of the best holidays we ever had. And to think we were in a wide age range, from our young teenage daughters to David Webber, who was in his 65th or 67th year, and we'd all managed this wonderful journey. Going back to their ranch for the rest of our holiday, we eventually flew home, thanks to Patrick Henry, first class. Of course, the girls were in their element—travelling on a jumbo jet first class was quite something to them. We seemed to manage to pull off these sorts of holidays because of these wonderful American friends and their generosity.

Another year, Gaby and I decided we would like to go up into Colorado to see cowboy country. We had some other friends that had a chalet of about ten bedrooms in Aspen, Colorado, and Pete and Mary-Lou, our friends from Scottsdale down in Phoenix, decided that they would meet up with us. So the holiday was just a typical tourist's holiday. We went to Denver, then to Salt Lake City. We kept to small-town roads, really, looking and seeking out the beautiful little old towns in the gold mining country, where the settlers had had their dig-outs. There was, in fact, still one gold mine operating, and a lovely train ran right through the valley, which was a lovely experience.

We'd heard about these cowboys and we'd seen them in the bar in town. They really were cowboys and the bars catered for them. I've never seen such a size! I mean, 50 people could sit at the bar, and they would order their drinks like you see on the films: a bottle would be put in front of them and they'd drink what they wanted and then pay for it all at the end. Then they'd get in their jeeps instead of getting on their horses, and go back to their working ranch. However, we still wanted to see the cowboys at work, so we went into Silverton, where the High Street was just as it was in the olden days. We went into the bank to ask for some help, and the bank was still as it was in wild west times, with iron grilles and counter service, as you see in John Wayne films.

We said, "Is the manager about?" and they said, "Yes, we'll just go and get him." I think it was strange for them to see two English people in the bank asking for the bank manager. Anyway, he kindly showed us into his office and we asked him what the possibility was of us seeing any cattle and real cowboys at work.

He got on the telephone and had a conversation. We didn't hear the other side, but he smiled at us when he put the phone down and said, "You are in good luck."

The Ralph Lauren ranch was bringing down 1,000 head of cattle that very afternoon, and we would be most welcome to go up to the ranch. Well, it was such an enormous surprise for us to be invited to this absolutely magnificent ranch house and estate, where all the cowboys lived and worked. We did actually see the drive coming down the mountains and being brought into Ralph Lauren's estate ready to be shipped off to market. The drive was so big, and they were bringing down so many head of cattle, that it would have taken hours, so we ended up being up there for ages before they were all in, and gradually the time came for us to say goodbye. We have memories that still live today, and there's a lovely photograph of Gaby sitting on the railings of this ranch house.

I talked about this railway that went down the valley, and took the best part of half the day. We tried to book, but unfortunately failed to get on it. Well, that night at dinner Pete said, "Well, there's always two ways of skinning a cat," but I didn't really know what he meant, and looked at him quizzically.

He said, his eyebrows arching, knowingly, "There'll be a surprise in the morning."

The morning came, and as we had breakfast, he said, "Well, we're going to go down the train route." We didn't quite understand what he meant, but he said, "I've got the jet outside."

We were going to go down the valley in his private jet! So that was beautiful. We flew over all the beautiful Colorado countryside, and then he suddenly picked out this train in the distance. He had been a fighter pilot in the war, so he knew exactly what he was doing as he suddenly banked and dived down towards this train. Poor Gaby really felt quite sick, and it took its toll for a while. We flew down, as if it was a James Bond film special effect, diving down the valley and picking up the train, just a few hundred feet above it, until we were following it down the valley. So we saw what we would have seen on the train, except from Pete and Mary-Lou's private jet. That just shows the sheer generosity of these American guys!

Of course, in some instances we were able to repay our debts when some of our hosts came over to England. Patrick Henry and his wife, Anne, used to come over. He was the Head of American Airlines, if you remember, and they would stay with us in the hotel. One of our hunting guys came over and spent a couple of days hunting with me, which was sheer exhilaration for them because they're hardly used to any jumps at all in their terrain, whereas we had all these hedges. It was very exciting for the guy!

So, all these holidays and meeting various people around the world, was a tremendous reward for the work I put in with Best Western. I was on the board for some time and was instrumental in the merger of Europe and America, so I was used to being treated as a high-powered executive. Yet I still had my lovely business at home.

We had a fabulous holiday on safari with the children when they were young, and that stayed with us because we paid extra to have our own guide, so of course were able to stop whenever we felt like it. We stayed down in the Serengeti National Park to start with, for nearly a week, because it was so luxurious and there was so much to do. The children were delighted with it and always wanted to go back, but somehow we never seemed to manage it; other holidays came in the way. We went to Mombasa for a sunshine holiday, but we didn't do safaris again.

The next most popular holiday, by a long way, was going to Mexico. We had a friend who owned two or three very luxurious hotels in Mexico, so we flew in direct from London to Mexico, where he collected us and we stayed with them for a few days, then went off up the Pacific coast because I didn't want 'the Blackpool side', as I call it. We spent a week driving around the old colonial towns and came back to the

Camino Real hotel. I loved this little old town, a tourist town in every sense and very busy, but there are so many restaurants it's hard to decide where you want to go. So in the end Gaby and I had three years of holidays in Mexico and I would go again, but at the moment, I've not picked up the courage to fly all that way in my current state.

The other great holidays we had were in Thailand—we went there three times. It was with some friends one year; we stayed down there in Phuket at the yacht club, which was still small and private. That was heavenly and so peaceful. We went to see a show in the main town, which was so beautiful and all the girls were so well dressed up, that I went up to the stage to hug one of them, and of course this was hilarious to the rest of our group of friends, because they were Thai ladyboys, but I didn't realise it. So I got caught out!

We always went into Bangkok and stayed at the Shangri-La Hotel on the banks of the Mekong River, because we liked it. It was very expensive but very luxurious. Another year we went, it was completely the opposite, again through Best Western. One of the other great holidays was from the sublime to the ridiculous. Every year there's a trade fair of international tourism held in London, and all the countries of the world take their stands. Best Western had its own big stand, so I got to know the sales director of a group of hotels in Thailand.

We had decided, with his help, that we would go on a trekking holiday with a difference, because neither of us can walk too far, especially Gaby. We decided that we would fly up to the middle of Thailand in the north, and two guides would meet us who'd already been briefed on what we wanted to do, which was rather adventurous to say the least. I wanted to trek into the real countryside of Thailand, where the people live without any involvement in tourism, and we chose to go by river, finding the various rivers that flowed northwards towards the Mekong Great River. We set off going west, where you couldn't go by river and were more or less in the forests and the agricultural countryside of Thailand, where everywhere was verdant green, growing vast amounts of vegetables, but there was no river. So, for this part of the journey we always travelled by elephant. It took a bit of getting used to, I can tell you, more for Gaby than for me because of my experience horse riding. But nevertheless, it was tiring and somewhat strange to stride along on an elephant who would push his way through wherever we needed to go—this is why they were chosen, really. We would reach the river, and maybe stay the night, before setting off on the next part of the journey.

There were no hotels, so we stayed with Thai families. I'm sure you can imagine, this was an absolutely incredible experience, being totally cut off from what you're used to, totally in the wilds, sleeping with a Thai family in their wooden huts raised up from the ground away from the animals and for the monsoon period. So we quickly had to get used to sleeping in our bunks or in the gear we'd taken with us, and we quickly had to get used to dining as a member of their family. I have to say, because the food is so fresh and abundant, and we adore Thai cooking anyway, we managed to do this for the next two weeks. And we never had a funny tummy or a mosquito bite; we were advised to go in March when it's more or less the dry season and the female mosquitoes don't come out.

The next day we would pick up the boat that we had hired and we went down all the rivers on these long tailboats—you've undoubtedly seen them, these big, long, canoe-shaped boats, which would carry about four people, with a big lorry engine on the back. When you needed to, you could skim the water at a fair old pace, or you could just meander if you wanted to, and we did both. We were strictly warned that when we reached the Mekong River, we should not cross to the Burma side of the river because of the trouble that prevailed over there. So as much as we were tempted to, we never did.

One of the highlights was going to the long-neck village, halfway through our journey. Young girls have gold or copper rings placed round their necks, and as they grow, they add another one in order to stretch the neck longer. They're called the long-neck people, and they're very colourful. I was flabbergasted how clean everywhere was, even in the villages. There might be a dirt road or whatever, but it was kept spotlessly clean and the families were always dressed in highly colourful clothes, which were mostly made by the grandparents.

Eventually we met up with the Mekong River, and I'd never seen such a vast expanse of water. The river was like a lake, and the traffic going up and down it was so varied and interesting. There'd be quite a lot of Chinese barges going up and down with the wares that they were either exporting or importing. This excitement continued until we got to the end of our journey, because our visa didn't allow us to go further on, and we were met by car. The first thing we did was go to a hotel, soak in a bath and clean up before we even went ten yards in the car. And then we went back into Bangkok and on our way home. So that was the next most exciting holiday.

As the children were growing up older, the farmhouse we had in Wales really wasn't as appealing to them as it had been when they were smaller, and there was a lot of work to do on it. So I decided to sell it, and we replaced it by buying an apartment in Cannes in the South of France, overlooking the bay and set in these lovely gardens with a pool. We really had struck lucky in getting what we wanted, because it was so nice. We did a deal with a lady from Luxembourg, and we did all right because in France it works differently to England. Once you've said you want a place, you put down a fair slice as a deposit, and then if anything changes, you lose the deposit. What we didn't realise was that she was in the middle of a divorce, so this could not be settled because of the financial arrangements with the divorce procedures; but because the flat was so gorgeous, we didn't want to lose it and ended up having to wait a year for it. Anyway, we've had 20-odd years of fun, and Christine and her family and two boys go down now, and funnily they don't want to go anywhere else in the summer because they just love it. So we go down often. Before I had my accident, we had lots of long weekends there to get away from business.

Timeshares enter my life

In 1975, the hotel was starting to do very well again, but my attention was moving to other things. There was a company in Scotland that sold timeshares, which was quite a novelty then, and I was fascinated. Every time we went on holiday down to the South of France there were timeshares all over the place, and I was drawn to them like a magnet. Sometimes this irritated Gaby, because in the middle of our holiday I'd always be saying, "Oh, I just want to go and look at this timeshare," until I knew everything about timeshares, inside out.

So I had this bee in my bonnet that I wanted to sell timeshares in an establishment at home. The only trouble was, whilst it was legal in Scotland, it wasn't in England, and therefore we had to have the law changed first. I'd never done anything like this before, so I went with my accountant, Basil, and Robin Walker to see my solicitor, Alistair, and explained what I wanted to do. He got most excited about it all. Well, of course, he would, wouldn't he? Because he'd be getting a fat fee! But he also enjoyed doing the work, and they'd been my solicitors since we started the hotel.

We'd written to a barrister whom Alistair had chosen, with the brief we wanted to discuss and down we went into these plush offices in the City of London.

It's a bit unnerving to go down to Chambers for the first time, into a barrister's consulting rooms, but we were all made most welcome. We sat down, introduced ourselves, and explained what we wanted to do. Lo and behold, he started giving me a lecture on tourism in Britain! Well, they charge a very hefty fee by the minute, so I was getting more and more irate as this was this going on. So I said to him, "Well, I beg your pardon, your worship, but I'm better qualified to lecture you on tourism than you to me. It is, in fact, my job in life. We've come down to you for advice on a legal matter, and that's what I would like to get on with!"

Alistair hissed, "Oh John! He's a barrister!" as if I should calm down. Well maybe so, but he infuriated me so much!

The barrister shut up, things settled down and he got very interested in what we were trying to do in the end, promising to take the case on. So in due course, he worked through the legal system and eventually managed to get the law amended, to permit the same arrangements as Scotland. So we were jumping up and down in delight!

While this was all proceeding, we'd seen this gorgeous estate on the Mawddach Estuary, near Dolgellau, in Wales that would be ideal for our timeshare project. It was on a hill overlooking the river and the bay, and to us, was so idyllic that we just couldn't resist it. The family who owned the house had got into some financial troubles and needed to sell it, and my intention was to turn it into the hotel with a few rooms and dining, and to build 12 Norwegian log cabins in the grounds. We applied for planning application and planning consent, which everybody seemed to be enthusiastic about—so that was one stumbling block out of the way. We'd got the law changed, so that was all right, too. We even managed to raise the money, as well. So really, it seemed to be all systems go.

The architect was well prepared; we'd found a firm in Norway that would build these log cabins, transport them over and put them onsite, which wouldn't take too long. But by then we were into 1975; the Labour Government was in power, and they'd suddenly passed the 1975 Land Act, which meant that projects like mine had to be for the benefit of the local community. However, it was deemed that this was for the benefit of John Mawdsley, so they served me with a compulsory purchase order, and bought the estate back off me at the price I'd paid—which was fair enough. But of course, they did not pay me the cost of having the law changed, or for planning consent or any other costs; so I was considerably out of pocket and very annoyed at the same time, as you can well imagine. In the end, it benefited nobody, because nothing ever happened to it, and it lay empty for years and years. So that was the end of that escapade.

The idea of timeshares, however, never left me, and it returned in some years to come, as you will undoubtedly hear.

So, by '76, life was continuing to be hard work but enjoyable. I had started hunting, as I've said, to the great merriment of my whole family, especially for me and the children because they had their little pony and they came out with me on a lead rope. Which of course, was highly exciting for them. They were early starters in the riding world, but they became quite competent and gradually hunted with me for the rest of my life until, of course, my accident brought it all to an end.

It was a funny thing. They went up to the local riding school and worked there on Saturdays, mucking out, and playing with the ponies. This kept them out of mischief, gave them something to do, and they also learned to ride in a much more professional manner. I never wanted to send the children away to boarding school because I felt it had a detrimental effect on family life. I wanted them to enjoy being a young family at home and I think it proved to be the right thing in the end—for me, anyway—because my children grew up exceedingly well behaved, highly educated, and were nice young ladies.

So we all went out in the lorry, which of course I had to go and buy, and on a Saturday we were always together. One of the benefits of the lorry was that if there was ever any problem—which there always is in family life, especially with young children—any problems always got sorted out in the lorry. Don't ask me why, but in our travelling time, either I'd discuss with the children that they were not behaving well or were not working at school hard enough, or they'd say, "Daddy, will you help us with this, that or the other?" even with their boyfriends later on. So the lorry became a wonderful tool for family discussions and clearing any household problems.

So we did take notice of what the doctor had told me about getting a hobby. In fact, I think we did it in extravagant style, because the hotel was doing so well that I really wasn't short of any money. At one time, we had four horses in the stables at home and a full-time groom during the season, right until the days I decided to send them up to livery. So we had a busy yard, and in summer all four horses were out in the fields, sometimes playing, sometimes asleep, but it was such a lovely sight to see all these from the house. Our groom would often get a job in the hotel over summer, or a summertime job somewhere else and return to us for the hunting season.

I'd suddenly seen the opportunity of buying another hotel. By chance, one came on the market up in the Lake District of Great Britain, which is one of the most scenic areas in the country, and a highly desirable holiday destination. We saw this hotel called Crooklands, which was very accessible, near the motorway, and decided to buy it. It was a lovely old pub, and I liked it so much that I decided that it would really be a tremendous asset to the hotel company. It seemed so irresistible to me. It had been transformed beautifully into two separate bars, 20 rooms, two bars, a restaurant and brasserie, and did a lot of local business. So I decided to go ahead and buy it.

Chris Gabbot, my manager from Mollington, went up to manage it with his wife Barbara. He'd worked for me for many years and he came over from Liverpool with me, so I knew the hotel was in safe hands and

I'd have to recruit a new manager for the hotel down in Chester. It was just a lovely little pub, and Chris managed it with Barbara exceedingly well. It ran very smoothly and didn't take a lot of effort. I went up there maybe once a week, sometimes once a fortnight. I would go over the different things that they might want to change on the menus or the bar. There wasn't much expenditure or building works, it was just an ongoing business that we'd bought and it carried on running. It was so much fun. It was a lovely, typical English pub with rooms and Chris ran it exceedingly well, so we kept it for 10 years or more until we sold the business later on.

So we now had two hotels, both doing well, as was Interchange Hotels, so it was incredible how things had turned out.

So, we come to the early '80s, and my passion for hunting still continued. I was invited down as a guest, to the South Nottinghamshire Hunt, about 50 miles south of us. On the first day, I was invited into the house, I discovered there were two guests, myself and Prince Charles. I knew him anyway from my days at Clarence House, and from seeing him as a youngster playing polo in Windsor, so it wasn't as if we were strangers.

Well, it's customary when hunting for the guests to ride upfront together, so it was a wonderful opportunity because I'd not really seen Prince Charles since I'd left Clarence House, and then he was only a young boy. But he fully remembered who I was. He was tremendous fun and a very good horseman, so I was rather pleased I had my best horse out on that day.

We had a great morning of tremendous hunting over stone wall country, which terrified the pants out of me. Taking these walls, upfront, all cold-blooded, took a bit of nerve. Nevertheless, because my horse had come from that area, he just flew the walls. The biggest danger jumping in stone wall country isn't taking off, because you can see what you're doing; it's when you get the other side of the wall—you don't know what's on the ground. Often people have clipped the wall and knocked the top off, so stones are lying on the other side. If you land on one of those you'll come to grief, sure as God made little apples. But on that occasion, we didn't.

Prince Charles was an admirable huntsman and hunting was second nature to him. So we spent the day thoroughly enjoying ourselves, and when we got back to the house for drinks and hotpot, we were bantering away about team chasing. Team chasing is a sport that follows hunting at the end of the season, while farmers still allow you on their land. You have a team of four people, and the first three of the four that finish across the line is the winner. So it's a high speed, cross-country course; highly exhilarating.

We'd got on so well, that I said to Prince Charles, "You like team chasing, and I know you've got your own team. If I bet that me and my team would beat you on our ground in the Cheshire Forest, would you take a wager on?"

And he said, "Oh, I'd love to do that." and agreed to come up to the Cheshire Forest in February.

So Frank Mason, my architect, who also hunted with us, and David Whelan, owner of JJB Sports, joined our team, and we were set with three and we needed our fourth, which eventually we got. David was another fanatical hunting person who liked going over hedges and out of water, and always had a bet that whoever fell off paid each other £10.

The idea was that the team of four race round this cross-country course against the clock, and the best of the three going through gave you the time.

For some unknown reason, the night before, I suddenly changed the horse I was going to ride. The horse I'd chosen to ride was a very big, strong, Irish hunter, whereas the black horse I was originally going to ride was more of a gentle thoroughbred. I decided to ride my Bay, a bigger, stronger horse that took some handling. Don't ask me why. I will show you it was a very bad mistake.

Anyway, I was leading my team, in front of Prince Charles at that moment. We were coming down a steep hill, and the jump was over rather a big brook, with a bridge, and the obstacle was a big telegraph pole on the other side of the bridge.

As we approached, I realised you had to get on the bridge and then jump over the big telegraph poles laid the other side. Well, I couldn't check the horse hard enough as we were motoring along, because we were against the clock. I was going a little too fast for my liking, and he was such a powerful horse I couldn't get him under control properly.

The bridge was covered in shale, all black, and my horse thought he had to jump the whole of the bridge as well as the obstacle. He tried to take the whole lot at once, and took off in an enormous leap, but didn't quite make the other side properly. He clipped the top of the telegraph pole and we fell, rolling. He landed on top of me and was winded so badly he couldn't move, so I was trapped underneath the horse. A lot of people came running to help, and the race was stopped. Some of my friends got hold of the horse's legs and rolled him off me, called the ambulance, and I went to Chester Hospital.

I was sort of semi-conscious, I remember. Gaby and David Wade, the farmer who lived opposite, were in the hospital with me, concerned that no-one was attending to me. David said he wanted to see the registrar, which seemed to take an age, and when he arrived, we had a row. So Gaby said, "Right, we're going to go to the Nuffield private hospital where we're going to get some proper service!"

Luckily enough, I was covered by BUPA, so an ambulance was arranged and I was transferred to the Nuffield, where they called out one of the best orthopaedic surgeons in the country. He said I had severely broken my pelvis, so there was going to have to be a fairly long operation in which he wired each of the breaks. Then they put weights on the end of my leg in order to keep the pelvis in a straight position while the bones set, which was going to take some six months of me lying on my back unable to move. And by God, he was right—it took close on six months in hospital.

Good comes out of bad

I was bored stiff in hospital.

But good always comes out of bad, funnily enough. Because I was in a private room, I could do what I wanted within reason. So it was then, in about 1980, that I got bored and started to get my secretary to come in daily. I had to do something, as I was itching to work, so I had the staff coming into the hospital as though it was my office. Good job the BUPA hospitals don't mind this. Anyway, one day, Basil Mitchell, came in. He had been my accountant from the day we started business— we were both the same age and he had just embarked upon his own company of accountants, and he was doing very well.

I said to him, "I don't really think I want the hotel when I get back. I think I'll sell it."

He was rather puzzled by this and said, "Why do you want to sell a good ongoing business?"

"I have to follow the industry, otherwise I'm going to be left behind."

"So, what is the industry doing?" Basil asked curiously, wondering what I meant.

I said, "The big boys like Holiday Inn are all putting pools onto their hotels to entice the customers to come for the weekend. And they're exceedingly successful." I said, "This is what is needed, and I can't do it. So I think we'll put the hotel up for sale, because I don't think I can keep up with the big boys with all their swimming pools and spas."

"What's your problem, then?" he said. "Well, you said you're bored, and you've got nothing better to do. Why don't you make plans to redevelop the hotel you've got? You may as well sit down and design it. Then you can go for planning permission and sell the hotel with that, if you really want to. It will add a lot of value to it."

So that gave me a great incentive to start designing what I thought a modern day hotel required, bringing the hotel up to 80 bedrooms. I completely planned to demolish the lounge and bar area and have that all rebuilt, in conjunction with a new restaurant. Two of the most contemporary leisure clubs—one was Gleneagles—had the most spectacular swimming pool and spa, with a restaurant that overlooked the pool. The only problem was, if you were eating in the restaurant you smelt the chlorine fumes from the pool, which always put me off. So I stated in my design that I would like the pool to be chlorine-free if at all possible.

When I came out of hospital, Basil said, "Now you've got this far, why don't we build it ourselves?"

I looked at him, askance. "But I don't have that kind of money, Basil!"

"Leave it to me," said Basil, with a firm nod, as if anything were possible.

Well, this gave me enormous exhilaration, but also enormous fear, because what I'd designed was for one of the big boys who had the money. It took me another year to do the feasibility study and appoint the architects to properly design what I thought I wanted, until we got the rough calculation of the cost. I got rather a shock that it came out at close on two million—and this was back in '83/'84. I didn't know how I was going to raise that sort of money, but Basil wasn't terribly put off.

It was quite some sum of money—or it certainly was to me. I know the hotel had grown and I know we were highly profitable, but nevertheless . . . Basil was determined that we wouldn't borrow the money from the normal banks. He said, "We won't go for conventional borrowings on this scale, because it's too risky." He said, "If there's any smell of the economy getting into difficulties, like we had in the '70s, they'd be calling the money back and that would put you in a rather precarious position. We'll do it the way the Germans to their banking." He said, "Don't worry. We will borrow what the bank will agree to lend us and I think we need to go into partnership with an equity company."

We chose ICFC, which was rather a large organization that lent money to entrepreneurs to grow their businesses. They would have a stake in the business, which they would either keep or sell when the business was very profitable; that's how they made their money. Anyway, we did a deal. They took 17.5 percent of the company, and then we borrowed the major proportion of money from them.

We were still short, so Basil came up with the idea of offering preference shares for sale to the local general public. He got that off the ground, and it was fully subscribed very quickly. By now, we'd raised most of the money—we were just £100,000 short. So I pestered and pestered the Tourist Board for a grant, and in the end, we got it. We now had all the money in place and decided that we'd go ahead and take the risk of building. By this time, I think I owed more money than the business was worth; especially until we'd finished the whole complex.

The actual cost was £2.5 million. That was already enough for me in 1983! We finished the basic design and then we had a model made so that I was sure of what I was going to get. I think you can see better from models. I didn't worry about staffing it yet because there was so much to do and the building was going to take over two years. So we were starting work in 1983.

We were building the bedrooms on the left side of the hotel and the gardens, and the leisure club on the right hand side. So everywhere you went, there were builders. We had designed a gym, beauty salons, two squash courts and a restaurant—quite a large restaurant, really.

As I've said before, I prided myself in the gardens and we employed three gardeners, so you can imagine the sheer beauty of a garden tended by three gardeners. There was a very large rhododendron garden that must have been 100 years old; the sizes and shapes were so heavenly. Within the first few weeks we were setting out the plot, as one normally does. The lounge was to be rebuilt first, then the bedrooms, and finally we would start on the leisure club. But because the previous owners wanted the gardens to be seen from the house, the lounge was right in the middle of them. So, the bulldozers arrived to demolish part of the old house in order to make this beautiful new lounge and glass veranda. We had boarded the lawn to protect it from the heavy machinery. We unfortunately had to pull all the roses out and fill in the sunken garden, which was all right—I knew that was happening and I was prepared to make a new rose garden.

But I went to London for the day for a meeting with Interchange Hotels and when I came back, my entire rhododendron garden been ripped up by the bulldozer! Well, I'm sorry to say that the first thing I did was burst out crying, because they'd ruined some of the pride and joy we had, and a century of growth. I totally lost my temper with the clerk of works and the architects, because it had been quite clearly laid out on paper what was to be retained, and where, so they should not have made any mistake. We'd already contracted a firm of landscape gardens to manage the garden scheme, just as we had the building scheme. But there you are—it had gone, and no way could we get it back.

The lounge took a relatively short period of time. We extended it, trebling the size of the lounge and we'd installed a huge log fire. Everybody who came in was thrilled with what we'd done, with a brand new bar and slick bar staff who knew how to shake a cocktail. And I have to say that this big glass veranda that you could walk along was stunning. It followed into the restaurant, and the views of the garden and the Welsh hills beyond were absolutely gorgeous. It just transformed the whole area, because it ran into the front hall and the entrance, where we'd created a brand new reception counter and office, so the whole of the entrance that greeted you on arrival gleamed with a sort of beauty, so delightful on the eye. And because it did reflect my background in quality hotels with no shadow of a doubt, for once in my lifetime, I began to say we were well on our way to creating a four star hotel—which is, of course, what I wanted.

Next came the bedrooms, which took about a year to complete. They were basically all identical apart from two suites at the end, and as up-to-date as I could imagine within the realms of bedrooms at that time. Since then, I've built the Big Blue Hotel in Blackpool and the Smith's Hotel in Gretna Green, where the interior design used is completely different and a far cry from what we did back in '83, looking back now, but nevertheless, it was in the most contemporary style at the time.

So, we were slowly making progress. All those areas were finished, and we re-laid the lawns, and fenced off the garden from the spa so we could get on with making the garden look more like a garden. Because a great garden takes so long to mature, we didn't want any more mishaps.

The builders came in to set out the site of the leisure club and began to dig the hole for the swimming pool. But what with their cabins, the construction site area and the buildings in a state of upheaval, whilst it was extremely exciting to see it started, it was really horrifying to look at. Meanwhile, I was still trying to run a hotel without the customers complaining too much.

The pool was 17.5 metres in length and 14.5 metres in width, so it was a good-sized pool. And this is where one of the problems occurred, since, if you remember, I said I wanted it chlorine-free.

I went to Gleneagles with Gaby, to conduct some research particularly on their leisure club. We decided to copy some of their ideas: the shape of the pool, and some of the planting and rocks. We stayed in the hotel and ate in the restaurant quite a lot at lunchtime because they had a lovely menu serving nice, light meals that were very well executed. But something disturbed me, since it was a pleasure eating except for the obnoxious smell emanating from the swimming pool the restaurant overlooked.

So I said, "For goodness sake, we can't have a smell like that. I don't want any chlorine fumes at all in our pool."

Well, nobody knew how to achieve this until I met a company called S.I. Sealy of Manchester, who had done some work for King Fahad of Saudi Arabia, at his palace. I had a friend who was a secretary to the Sultan of Oman, and because it's always one person who knows another, he got me the introduction to King Fahd's empire and we wrote to the estate. We explained we'd heard that he'd succeeded in creating what was called a micro-climate, and we were fascinated to know more. He allowed us to go out and see for ourselves what it did, so, we flew out to see it.

Well, honestly, this was so exciting, going out to Arabia, and when we got there we were very well received. The only drawback was that we'd worked out a timetable and had forgotten entirely how life works over there. You might make an appointment on a Tuesday, but you wouldn't actually get to meet with the person or see what you'd arranged to see until Wednesday, Thursday or Friday, so you just had to hang around. It didn't matter, because they looked after you in the most luxurious fashion, but it was fairly frustrating, nevertheless, not to be able to get on with doing what we wanted to do! But we didn't complain too much because we were being spoiled.

When we did get to see the pool system, well, blow me down—he actually had an oxygen plant in the pool room generating pure oxygen that was injected into the pool. Well, oxygen is one of the biggest anti-bacterial agents there is, and of course, there is no smell and no taste. In fact, if anything, it was slightly salty. Between the pool and other areas there was also the system of an air curtain to stop the two airs mixing with each other, created by a thermal wall. The restaurant level was slightly higher than the pool, with about 20 ceiling fans blowing air towards the pool at varying speeds, controlled by a small computer. When this air met the air from the pool, it caused a curtain, because the cooler air dropped to the floor and no smells came into the restaurant.

I was so elated! I came back inspired and we said to S.I. Sealy, "Now we've seen what's been done and how to do it, that's what we want to do!"

So, with S.I. Sealy's we designed a micro-climate, which was very clever. Along the whole back wall of the complex, on the restaurant side overlooking the pool, we built air ducts right across the span of the ceiling from the end of the restaurant to where it met the sloping gangway, down this lovely, non-slip tiled floor to the pool some 15 feet below the restaurant. At the end of these ducts little fans, about 18 inches wide, controlled by a computer, were calibrated to work at different speeds and create the air flow at different points on the balustrade of the restaurant. As this blown, cooler air met the warm air from the pool complex, the air dropped, causing a thermal barrier. Therefore, no smells from the restaurant entered the swimming pool, and nothing from the pool came into the restaurant. So we had achieved our first major objective in innovative construction: something nobody else had anywhere in the west.

My other aversion to swimming pools is chlorine, the major smell that entered the restaurant at Gleneagles. It always clings to your clothes or your body, as well as offending your nose and making your eyes smart. So again, I said to S.I. Sealy, "We've got to come with another idea or method of controlling the bacteria in the pool."

He said, "Well, that's not quite so difficult as your previous demands. I think I know somebody in Scotland that manufactures different plants, so we'll go up and see him."

So off we trotted, on another adventure, to a firm in Glasgow that did, in fact, deal in different methods of controlling bacteria in pools. There were several different solutions to use rather than chlorine, the

ultimate of which—just designed—was an oxygen plant that created
your own pure oxygen which was then injected into the pool. The pool
becomes as sweet as any water you could find. I said, "Well, that's it!
That's just what we want! Everybody will be overwhelmed. There'll be
no smell, no sore eyes and certainly nobody, even the likes of Holiday
Inn, have got this. We'll be able to boast about all these innovations."

So we'd achieved all that, at a horrendous cost of £100,000—but
never mind. It was what I really wanted, and it would be the talk of the
industry for years to come.

As the pool was being finished, I wanted mosaic terrazzo tiles in the
pool, but the quotes we were getting were forbidding. But I think you've
got to know my character now—I never really give in if I can help it! I
managed to find a local tiler in the village, and went to see him at home
saying, "How would you like a year's work or more doing all my work at
the leisure club?"

He jumped at it. He worked on his own, and he wasn't fast, but
he was meticulous in his work, and eventually the pool began to look
something like a pool. I wanted an image of a big dolphin on the
bottom of the pool and one of my directors, who was an artist as a
hobby, designed one for me which covered the whole pool, really, which
was created in mosaic tiles. Then, at last, we got the fire brigade to come
and fill the pool, little by little, so that none of the tiling was damaged.

So, we had encountered hurdles, but I was unwilling to compromise
on quality, although these hurdles were beginning to cost money. I had
all sorts of extravagant ideas coming out of my head, and poor Frank
Mason was overwhelmed by all that I wanted done and the amount of
money we were spending.

Then I had this idea that in the entrance of the leisure club,
running through into the restaurant, I wanted all the walls to be marble
to make it really look luxurious. Having had a stepfather with a marble
business and my brother now running it, I told Richard I wanted an
exotic marble.

"I want a marble wall like you get in these grand, plush banks. I want something very different. The theme is green—we're going to have different shades of green in the carpets."

So he said, "Right, let's fly out to Carrara and go and see one of the merchants I know. Then we'll go looking for the sort of marble in the mountainside that you might like."

We flew out to Carrara, in the Tuscany region of Italy, where all the quarries have existed since the days when Michelangelo chose his marble from that area. Well, I thought this was most exciting, going off to get my own marble. We found the most gorgeous green with a gold vein in it—I was so elated with it. I chose what I wanted, and we got the block down, the block arrived in England, went down to Richard's firm, and they began cutting it up into slabs. So this was kept to one side in Richard's yard while the rest of the work was carrying on, until we were ready for it.

I didn't intend to advertise and promote the hotel and the new facilities. I aimed to attract attention and clients through excellent and sustained Public Relations. My PR lady, Rosemary Dunwich, whom I'd employed to cover the whole of the construction of the opening, was drip-feeding the press about what I was up to. She was a master at making stories out of things she learned I was doing. This was a great story for her, so when some slabs of the marble arrived, she got one of her glamorous girls showing a leg on the marble. It was great as a photo-call for the press, and the story that I'd gone looking for marble like Michelangelo went out.

It was this beautiful, very pale green, naturally gold mottled in all sorts of shapes, and it was fabulous. We had it on all the walls of the entrance, all the way up to the restaurant. And I have to say, it really did look very exotic.

We had no more money, so in the end we had to say we've got to start doing a bit of saving. We ended up by saying, "Well, we'll get these things done and we'll penny-pinch on the changing rooms and corridors at the back." So we built them in breezeblock and we just painted them nice colours and left them at that, knowing we could tile them at some later date. That saved us quite a lot of money, so we were all very chuffed about getting back on track.

Rosemary was one of the best PRs I've ever come across and was a little devil at obtaining information. She had a weekly meeting with me, just to update her on what we were doing. Then she would find other things out and come to me saying, "John, you never told me about this!" Of course, she went around talking to the staff and the builders, and she found things out for herself and wrote her own stories of this hotelier creating an outstanding leisure complex attached to his hotel, the first in England to do it.

So, slowly, 1986 was beginning to dawn on us and we were getting near to finishing. The normal rat race occurred because we'd actually put a date on the opening, and it was like a madhouse—so many different trades, on top of everybody else trying to get their work done.

Never mind, to the credit to McAlpine's the builders whose contract it was, they managed to complete more or less on time and slightly over-budget, which our quantity surveyor managed to whittle down. So I was proud to say that the whole complex, with three different parts, was built on time and built to budget, and I give that credit to myself and my little team. There's not very many people can boast that.

Chapter 18

Interchange becomes worldwide

During the construction of the hotel, and throughout '83 to '86 really, the other things in my life didn't stop. David Baird-Murray of Llandrindod Wells had been Chairman of Interchange, and we had an arrangement by which we worked closely in France with Pierre de Devauchelle. We had met the Chairman of Best Western in America, and we'd made loose arrangements through that meeting in a bar in Amsterdam with Best Western. Would you believe it: two chairmen, two organisations in this tiny bar in one of the streets in Amsterdam—and the meeting resulted in us more or less agreeing to become Best Western and losing our identity as Interchange.

Around about 1983, whilst we were beginning to start building, I was asked to take on the role as Chairman of Interchange. Well, I had a lot of soul-searching to do and discussing it with Gaby over dinner for several days. At this time, I was heavily involved with building the hotel, and as you can imagine, the scale of the work took me a lot of time at home. I had many worries and concerns about this, and had several long conversations with Gaby about whether or not I could possibly do my building work *and* look after my other interests *and* be Chairman of Interchange.

On the Interchange front, it was really a huge success story, it had now grown to close on 200 members and our offices were now fully staffed with over 50 people selling different products for us and running advertising campaigns; not to mention our growing alliances in the United States and Europe.

The honour of being Chairman of Interchange now that it had reached such proportions was very great, and I could see the benefits of being Chairman of such a prosperous organization: it would undoubtedly do me and the hotel a lot of good. In the end, through discussion with Gaby, and being a glutton for punishment, I decided that yes, I would take it on. I was already Chairman of the Marketing Committee and I understood how Interchange worked. My dream of bringing a chain of hotels comparable to Trusthouse Forte to Great Britain was being realised, and I knew that being chairman and leading a company that size would do me an enormous amount of good, personally. The number of contacts you make when you're a chairman is enormous; I'd be suddenly thrust into the seat of a very powerful organisation, and I would travel very considerably. So, I decided to accept. It meant me travelling up and down to London quite frequently and chairing board meetings which stretched to two days at a time. However, it did put my hotel in good standing. I thoroughly enjoyed the role and so did Gaby.

Two or three years before, we'd met Pierre, who had this hotel in Fontainebleau; and they had a similar organisation in France to Interchange. Then we found that Germany's consortium was beginning get off the ground. We had already made loose arrangements with Best Western in America, who had got a vast number of hotels and a big organisation down in Phoenix.

Pierre and Jeannine became extremely good friends of Gaby and I, and Michael and Jean Webb. He decided that he would host a European convention in April 1984 for people from different countries we'd managed to encourage to be loose partners. We held this convention in Paris, and Pierre pulled out all the stops,

The 60 of us in the British contingent decided to go to France on the Orient Express, so we really didn't half set off in style! An experience on that train really is something of the glory of the past. The sheer quality of the train itself, which had been refurbished from its original, and the staff and cuisine were quite exceptional. The whole journey was so memorable, to this day. The train has a bar on it, and a piano, and of course, after dinner we managed to get the pianist to play once again. And I don't know, but somehow it broke into a singing contest. I don't think anybody went to bed that night! So we started off our 1984 convention in a real state.

Returning to Paris with my wife and our new agenda was really quite exciting. For the state banquet that Pierre had arranged for some 200 hoteliers from various parts of Europe, somehow he had managed to persuade the French Government to open the Palais de Versailles for the evening as our banqueting venue. So after the journey across from England we had our state banquet in the absolutely luxurious surroundings of the palace, full of French history and tradition. That really was something that very few people get the chance to do, and miraculously, Pierre pulled this all off! Well, it was an unbelievable occasion, being held in such a prestigious palace in France, especially opened for us, and the menu was composed of the best French food available. Those who attended that evening still talk about it today.

Then we had two or three days of different programmes about marketing on a European scale, trying to expand our joint countries into one European nation.

Now that I was Chairman, I seemed to go down to London more often, usually on the very early train on Monday morning, when we still had the beautiful breakfast service whereby they served you a full English breakfast, all fired from the galley and served in the First Class compartment. It was always packed. It seems a shame that today, all you get now is some damp bap put in the microwave. I'm just thinking fondly of the old days.

I'd go to the central office building, in which I had my own office, because I insisted upon it. I told Tony Rothwell, who was the Chief Executive, that my style of work might be different to other people's, but he was not to take any offence. I just had to feel like part of the working team- which is different to what a lot of big companies have, but I did not want to be a sort of external chairman. We had employed about 70 staff at least, and when I arrived at about half past nine in the morning until I arrived upstairs an hour to an hour and a half later, I would go through the building from floor to floor, seeing the heads of each department and having a good chat to find out what was going on, what was doing well, and what difficulties we had, like you would normally do in any business. I kept telling Tony I wasn't trying to go behind his back, even though I was supposed to just get the information I wanted from him. I knew from past experience that if I'd left it at that, he would have told me what he wanted me to hear; whereas by going round the business on my own, I found out in my own way; then I chatted to Tony about how and what we were doing.

It was during this time that we had formal discussions with Best Western in the States, flying back and forth to their headquarters in Phoenix, this glorious although very hot area of the United States, where we got to know their board of directors very well and became friends. We used to stay there for about three days, where we'd work round the offices, and since they already had something like 2,000 American hotels, their offices were vast. Because they had a call centre for booking business travel or tourism holidays, they had their own purchasing department, too.

We had more or less agreed to amalgamate towards the back end of 1985, and we had the final arrangements in place to make a presentation at the Best Western Annual Convention. I've told you how fabulous these conventions were and how much fun they made them. They do have good working sessions, but they also play very hard. So we were in Washington in October 1985, when we were to ratify the agreement. We were still negotiating with the American board and with the Europeans from The Netherlands, France, Germany, Spain and Italy, with the same type of organisation as we had in the UK, although they were about 40 hotels. We had to sit down, and I was particularly sensitive that although we were merging with the States, we were to have control of our own destiny, our own business. We had persuaded the rest of the Europeans that we wanted to do this and they all agreed unanimously, so it was fairly critical in the negotiations that Best Western pull this off to determine how it was going to run as one company.

A calamity arose during the negotiations. The German chairman pulled a dirty trick, and went to the American board behind our backs, caving in and saying that they were happy to sign the contract without the strict requirements that the British and French required. So this split the deal, and I remember to this day, both Pierre and I, who were really heading up this deal with America, had the most almighty row with the Americans. We were absolutely fuming because the Germans had stabbed us in the back, so we had no option but to tell the Americans that the deal was off and we were leaving to go home. This was catastrophic for them, because they had lobbied all their American hotels and were going to present it at the conference. As far as they were concerned, the deal was done and dusted; except they had thought we would climb down and come under their control like the American hotels, but that was totally unacceptable to us. In the end, we both said we wouldn't sign the contract, left the room and went out to dinner with our wives.

Well, in the end, they capitulated, and on the 24th of October 1985, I stood on the stage to give the European presentation to the American delegates. We had put together a very startling presentation for this big stage, explaining why we wanted to amalgamate with the Americans. I was to make the presentation in front of all these people, and I really was quite nervous, especially since I wasn't feeling very well because we'd had a big dinner and party the night before and I'd eaten a bit too much lobster. I think some of it disagreed with me. Anyway, I know I didn't feel my best, and I wondered how I was going to get through it all. The Americans are past masters at these stage productions.

When I went on stage to stand at the podium, all of a sudden, unbeknown to me, a big halo of light came down and surrounded me, making it look as if I was going to be abducted by aliens and beamed up into the mother ship. I was unaware that this was how it was going to start, and I think the delegates were also dumbstruck by the vision. They played our country's national anthem, and then I gave my presentation. Afterwards, at a board meeting, I signed the contract, and that made us into Best Western Hotels Worldwide—the biggest hotel organisation in the world.

So, it was all a far cry from the 1960s to the 1980s. In 20 years we had gone from two hotels to over 2,000; from nothing to the largest hotel organisation in the world. It was fairly wonderful. And what were even more wonderful were the touring programmes we'd developed. Well, they had really grown and taken off. We created a brand called Getaway Holidays, which now meant that you could get away to over 2,000 hotels worldwide. The marketing appeal of this suddenly attracted some fabulous companies: American Airlines was the first and biggest deal we did, with Patrick Henry. Patrick Henry was the Chief Executive of their inbound traffic; he wanted to put the Getaway Holiday programme out with all their American marketing, and it was a huge success. They were able to sell holidays anywhere in the world with a single phonecall to a call centre in Phoenix, and the reservations system we had created with the latest technology meant that the girls were able to give the client instant replies, which had not happened anywhere in the world until that period. We had a film on all the American Airlines planes, flying from any airport to England. Of course, this was absolutely marvelous for us, because it meant we were gaining a lot of American business, which we would otherwise not have been able to attract.

Now that I was Chairman, I had to attend the American board meetings, which were once every two months, lasting three days.

I made many, many friends, and if I stayed at the board meetings for three days I invariably stayed over for the weekend. The hospitality of the American guys was fabulous to say the least: I don't know what it is about them, but they have the capability of making more money than my British compatriots, somehow. American hotels are taxed considerably less and they have big advantages on their property, so with the different systems and tax regimes, they were able to offer the client much cheaper accommodation.

So, finally, McAlpine's finished this beautiful complex on time and fractionally over budget, which we negotiated with them at the end of the contract. There were a few small areas I had to compromise on because I wanted these exotic things with a set amount of money; but we would do things like the changing rooms' walls properly, out of profits, in the future.

Chapter 19

The boldest move I have made

So, in 1986 the entire Molly B had reopened with its magnificent extensions, and I have to say it really did look sensational; the old and the new blended well. We'd had the gardens especially re-landscaped by a garden designer who was a professor at Liverpool University, so everything looked absolutely perfect.

We never advertised whatsoever, just had Rosemary doing PR stories, and holding PR cocktail parties to attract leisure club members to join. It didn't take very long for us to reach the 700 membership, which was into the profit zone. The membership flooded in because it was February and it was cold, which helped, because people wanted things to do.

We were well staffed and we had some lovely people in the reception office, lovely girls downstairs, and the beauty salon was extremely luxurious. Sue, a girl in her early thirties, was enticed by me to come up from London to head up this salon, and she chose Renée Enos products from Paris as fitting for this class of hotel. Not knowing anything about it, I agreed with whatever she said, and we ended up with a very first class beauty salon.

Later on—and this will make you laugh—I went down to see her and said, "Sue, I know all there is to know about how the hotel runs, and I am able to do anything I would ask a member of staff to do, but I'm in the dark in your department. That has to change. I need to know as much about the beauty salon as I do about the kitchen!" She blushed and started to laugh, but I said, "No, Sue. I'm deadly serious. I do need to know how it's run, what you do and how we're going to make money out of it."

So in due course, she taught me exactly what was required by ladies, what was required by men, how she went about it, and how she tried to balance the different demands of customers with helping the staff keep fresh during the day. No one can keep up doing massage all day long—they need to be able to have a rest—so they would do a lady's nails or eyelashes, something not quite so strenuous as massage. So they mixed and matched, and we worked seven days a week. We worked weekends flat out, because we offered a bridal service which was always snapped up immediately by the brides and their families. The whole beauty salon did nothing but prosper, and later on I had to enlarge it to make the hairdressing salon separate, and bigger.

The gym was fine. It was very large, with its own manager and nearly 50 different pieces of equipment. Each client had their own programme of activities and training sessions that he or she wanted to do. The squash courts took care of themselves, on a 'first come first served' basis to book the courts, and the members got their own squash league going, so that was good. The restaurant was running beautifully. Then we all needed training on the complex issues of how to operate the oxygen generator machine, balancing how much to inject in the pool, and how to keep the correct speeds going on the fans to keep the thermal barrier working. Alan Lester, who ran the pub, came over to manage the leisure club, and it all settled down very well.

We already had 700 members, and I was reluctant to let any more in at this stage because the last thing I wanted was it to be so over-crowded that people moaned that they couldn't swim or the changing rooms couldn't cope, so we kept it at that level. In fact, we kept it at that level for quite a few years.

The hotel had totally changed its character and its marketplace, and I said to myself and Gaby, "Now we've got a hotel of the standard I'm used to! Now, we can go forward."

I was going to challenge the Grosvenor, which was the Duke of Westminster's hotel in town, and I eventually got my four stars—which, as you can imagine, was thrilling. It was amazing for the Molly B to progress from a 12-bedroomed, no-star hotel to become four-star, and because of the leisure club, for it to be one of the foremost, most forward-looking hotels in England.

Rosemary, of course, had excelled in her work of PR, and the stories we kept getting were stupendous. We created our own club magazine, and this, once completed in 1986, was the dream that I could ever have wished for—to have a hotel that gained four stars, gained two AA rosettes for good food, and now was on a par with the Chester Grosvenor, but in a slightly different way.

Ours was set in the countryside and he was right in the heart of the city, so they were two different types, but I was so proud that I'd got a hotel that was equal to that of our sparring partner in golf, Richard Edwards, who was then the managing director of the hotel—and the Duke of Westminster who owned it, who I knew quite well, really, from various committees that I was on. Quite a lot of banter used to go— because now, for the first time in their lives, they had competition.

When it had all settled down, suddenly one day I got a letter saying I had been awarded the Queen's Award to Industry for Technical Innovation. Well, I couldn't believe my tiny eyes or ears when I read this. To get the Queen's Award for Industry was really quite something very special. After that we gained an award for Investors in People, so we were really clocking them up. We'd got the product, we now had to run.

You can see the sheer fun I'd had over three years and a bit more with planning, since my escapade with Prince Charles and hospital to now. With this product, suddenly a mediocre, three star hotel had become an exceptionally well known four star that attracted a totally different kind of clientele.

It's from there that I now leave you, and I will continue with the stories of what happened in the years to come. I have to say, I was still heavily involved with being Chairman of the Marketing Committee of Interchange Hotel, that is, Best Western, and I still had to go down to London on a very regular basis, and I had Crooklands and the College. But I had the most wonderful PA, Anne Fleet, who stayed with me for many years and became heavily involved how I ran the hotel. A person of that level of qualification and experience is an absolute, total gem to have with you, because she knows you almost as much as your wife knows you in their own respective ways. I wouldn't have got through it, or I would have struggled, without Anne. So I do pay credit to her as someone special in those years.

So, we let all this settle in, and it carried on making money for us.

During my chairmanship, it was decided that Great Britain would host the second European convention. Of course, as Chairman, that gave me extra responsibilities, and I really don't know how I had the stamina for all these things. I remember sitting in the conservatory, wondering how on earth it had all happened. I think had it not been for Ann Fleet, my PA, it wouldn't have done. She was so efficient, booking me into hotels and on flights to Europe and America, being involved with the extension; she was absolutely my right arm.

So, trying to match Pierre, who had already set a high standard, I was really racking my brain on where to go and what to do to top Versailles. Then, I had a flash of inspiration and announced at a board meeting, "Well, to match them, we need to go to the Guildhall!"

Everybody thought I had gone mad. How was I going to book a dinner into the at the Guildhall? But I made an appointment to go and see them and managed to persuade them that we were an international organisation, hosting the Europeans. To put Britain on its best footing, we would very much like to have the Guildhall. Well, they agreed! And then I racked my brain about who were we going to get as our main guests of honour.

Because of my connections with the royal family, I said, "Why can't we get Princess Diana's father and the Countess Spencer as our guests?"

Well, everybody once again thought this was a total impossibility. However, I wrote to them at Althorp Hall, explaining what I wanted to do, and I was invited over to discuss the possibility. And to my surprise, the Earl Spencer said yes and the Countess was overjoyed; in fact, she took control.

So, I'd organised most of things at the Guildhall and co-ordinated a menu, and then I got a message from the Countess Spencer to say she would like to have a tasting of the food before the event. So, here's a story you and all the readers are going to laugh at! I agreed to go down to the Guildhall and have lunch with her to see whether she liked what we had chosen. But it was the day before the Grand National. The Grand National for us, in those days, was the peak of our season. The number of racing people—and famous racing people—who stayed in the hotel for the period of the four or five days that the meeting lasted, and then all the punters who came over from Ireland; the whole place heaved and hummed with business.

We had a big fundraising dinner planned for that night with Bob Champion and Aldaniti. Jockey Bob Champion had already fought cancer and won the Grand National. Now, for charity, he was doing a sponsored ride and walk with Aldaniti from the south of England to Aintree Racecourse in Liverpool. He was going to stop with us overnight, stabling the horse in one of my stables, and was attending a charity fundraising dinner and a fashion show with us that evening.

So I made arrangements to go down to meet Countess Spencer and catch the train home, so that I'd be in good time for the evening's events. However, unbeknown to any of us, the weather turned very wild and the trains going down to London went very slowly. In fact, some of the lines adjacent to ours were not operating at all.

On my way, our train came to a stop, and the guard said, "We're held up for an unknown reason and for an unknown length of time."

People didn't have mobile phones in those days, so I asked the chief attendant to make a call for me to the Guildhall

The rail official looked at me as if I was insane. "I'm sorry, Sir. That can't be done. We aren't allowed to use our telephone service for the public's convenience. It's for British Rail business only."

"But I need to apologise to Countess Spencer! She's a member of the royal household."

"No exceptions, Sir. Not even for the Queen."

Well, he refused to do so, and I got really irate about this. "Not only won't you tell me when—or even IF—the train will be moving again!" I spat, incensed, "But you won't even arrange to send a message to Countess Spencer to say I can't get there!"

I would be standing her up for lunch without even sending a message—which to me was the most horrific impoliteness you could possibly imagine.

Infuriated, I had a row with the attendants, but they were implacable.

"Sod you!" I exclaimed, deciding that I was going to get off the train.

I flounced off, and opening the train door, stepped out into mid-air. There was quite a drop—which I didn't realise, because you don't notice it when the train is level with a platform. I had quite a jump to make to get to the ground. Well, the weather was howling outside, and there I was, in my best clothes, bowler hat and umbrella, with a slightly twisted ankle from my leap of faith, on the wet ground in the middle of nowhere.

So I set off, battling the wind with my umbrella up against the monsoon, tramping across the fields until I reached a small village. I asked someone for directions to anyone who had a taxi, or a phone so that I could ring Althorp Hall.

Ironically, it turned out that I was actually on the Althorp Estate, but the Countess would be in London by now. I just needed someone to get a message to her, and giving it all up as a bad job, I had to get back to Chester. I was directed to a small cottage where they said a taxi driver lived. I knocked on the door, which opened only two inches, and a beady eye scrutinized me from the narrow gap.

"I'd like a taxi, please. Someone said you had one?" I queried, slightly flustered.

They said, "He's out at the moment. Will you not come in?"

So I thought, "Well, it's far better to come in and keep dry than stay out here."

I went inside, and saw this grossly fat lady, I have to say, on the other side of the door, while this wafer-thin girl dressed in white sat gaping at me from an armchair.

I said, "All I want is a taxi to get to Chester."

"Well, my husband will be back shortly," she said, with an eerie grin. "While you wait, sit down and have a cup of tea,"

Which I did. I think that was a foolish thing to do, now. I sat down, and there they were, this girl and her, and the whole thing was so odd.

The thin girl wandered over to me, clutching her skirts and wafting them as she walked, her thin legs looking barely able to take the weight of her slight figure. "Do you like God?" she smiled.

"Well. We've never really met," I harrumphed, my eyes flitting to the fat woman, who wobbled towards me with a cup of tea. I grabbed it quickly and took a nervous mouthful, scorching the roof of my mouth.

Both of them grinned at me oddly.

"Would you like to come upstairs?" The obese woman said, with a glint in her eye. "Bethea will take you."

"No thank you," I gulped.

"We've got books," asserted the anorexic girl, her eyes wide. "We can show you things."

My eyebrows shot to my hairline. I suddenly had a terrible fear that the tea might be drugged, so I placed it down carefully on the old tea chest that sat next to me, which was covered in a lace doily.

"We're Jehovah's Witnesses . . ." began the fat woman, and then they were preaching to me that I should join their religious organisation—which was something of a relief to me at the same time as I was horrified by it. The whole experience in the house, this girl all in white and them wanting to get me upstairs—for what, I wouldn't know—unnerved me.

In the end, the door swung open, interrupting my brainwashing, and the husband arrived back home to save the day.

But when he walked in the room, he must have been about 75. I thought, "Oh, God forbid! Now what on earth's going to happen?"

I said, "I desperately need a car to take me to Chester."

Well, he looked at me as though I'd gone mad—because the hundreds of mile trip from Althorp to Chester was something he wouldn't normally dream of. Anyway, I persuaded him that I'd pay him well and we set off. Well, he squinted through the windscreen as if he was half blind, and I don't think we went more than 30 miles an hour. The whole time I was thinking, "Oh God, I'm not going to get there! Today's gone wrong so much already."

Anyway, I eventually got home just in time to get changed into evening dress and act as host for the charity ball, with Bob Champion bringing Aldaniti into the ballroom to everyone's surprise and cheers. And of course, the appearance of Bob Champion helped us raise £4,000 for his cause. After that, we then had a fashion show. Well, I don't know what I was thinking or why, but I must have given this some thought beforehand because I'd decided that I would get dressed up as a jockey for the fashion show, and one of the ladies, a sparkling girl, would also get dressed up in beautiful ladies' tails.

Well, I started chasing her up and down the catwalk, with my hunting whip out and I knew how to crack it very well. So I was galloping after her, cracking my whip at this girl. Well, the room fell apart, laughing and applauding, and photographs galore were taken of me. I had a lot of fun, and the whole evening ended up being 100 percent successful.

The next morning, Bob Champion and Aldaniti left the hotel, with plenty of photographers outside, for the last stage of his walk to Aintree Racecourse; where he rested the horse and rode in the Grand National that Saturday.

Things did get better. We never had the tasting with the Countess Spencer after all, because we couldn't get our diaries together. In the end she gave in and said, "Well, all right. Choose the menu. I'm sure you know what you're doing."

And indeed, we did!

Service Is Our Specialty!

Chapter 20

Beaujolais

As you know, having a privately-owned business gives one more flexibility and there's no-one to tell me when and what I can buy. Since the old hotel was built on a very early, pre-Victorian site and rebuilt at some stage, they kept all the beautiful cellars. So I got tempted to buy my own wine, lay it down for a year or two, and then sell it and make more money.

I was a bit of a wine fanatic, and I used to go over to Europe with Thomas Beatty, a big wine merchant at the top end of the market in Liverpool. I'd go along with him because he knew the areas well, knew the people concerned and the best vineyards. So, all our wines were bought directly from the country of origin, even the American wines. Again, through Thomas Beatty we got to know Mumm Champagne, which was owned by Seagram's, and we were invited out to visit Mumm or Seagram's in the Napa Valley, near San Francisco, to a very cheap winemaker (unbeknown to me), who made wine in quite a different way to the European style. He would get about three quarters of the way through the process, and if he wasn't happy with the wine he'd suddenly ring up one of the wine growers and say, "Can I have an extra so many hectares of grapes?" and then he would blend those into his

Champagne. And in doing that, it put up the cost of buying the wine, because he was buying small parcels just to get the wine right. He gave me the chance to try making my own, which was tremendous fun. Of course, the wine was a bit of rubbish really, because I certainly don't know how to make wine. I know how to taste it and love it, but not how to make it.

So, along with the buying of French wines, one of my trips every year was always to the house of Emile Chandesais. He lived near Nuits-Saint-Georges in the heart of Burgundy and had a vast vineyard just south of Beaujolais country. He had come up with an idea for promoting French wines, and in particular, the Beaujolais nouveau from the new year's pressing. One year I happened to be there with him and he said, "Have you never thought of entering the Beaujolais race?"

I told him I hadn't. So he explained, "Well, it's a wine race, leaving here at midnight and racing back to your establishment to get the Beaujolais nouveau served at your table. Whoever gets it home first is the winner and gets more press coverage than anybody else. However, the whole event, we have found, has been a very good publicity stunt for us at the House of Chandesais, and for you, the hoteliers. It's been going on for a few years."

He used to encourage people like me and some of the favourite restaurants—not only in England, but elsewhere in Europe or even Japan—to race to get their wines to their own country first.

I said, "Fine. When I get back to England I'll think about it."

So, when Ian Stubbings, my wine merchant from Thomas Beatty and Company, called, I discussed it with him.

"Oh," he said, "Oh yes, I know all about that. It's great fun, and it is a good publicity stunt, especially if you arrange to have a lunch party and the wine arrives in time for the lunch, or . . . in the extreme, fails to."

Anyway, I said, "Right, come on then, let's do it."

It wasn't particularly good wine in my eyes, but the publicity it created was fantastic, to say the least. The first Beaujolais Nouveau race we entered took place in early November—it varies every year depending on when the wine is ready, from early to mid-November. Through Ian, the wine merchant, and Jack Ferguson, the general manager of the Holiday Inn, we managed to borrow from the Liverpool City Council a 1942 Liverpool fire engine, still in working order, to our surprise. They said that we could borrow this fire tender if we advertised where it came from. The Fire Brigade checked this vehicle over thoroughly for us and six of us were set to go: Ian and me, Jack Ferguson, Neil Hall of Hall Brothers in Holywell. We also invited the BBC correspondent John Dunn to guarantee that we would get coverage on his show every afternoon. And the last person, I can't remember. The back of the fire tender was empty—like a van, I suppose—but we managed to persuade Gaby to get some eiderdowns and soft cushions for us to sleep on and so we could sit down in there during the day. So, all nicely furnished out, with food and drink, we set off from the hotel in good cheer and went on our way, down to Dover. Two of us sat in the front for driving, and four were in the back—we would each take turns driving every two hours. That way we kept everybody fresh, and those of us in the back had a good time—but of course, there was no drink at that point!

I had a great friend, Michel Bontot, who used to be my boss at the Georges V. He was now in Rungis, the town where the huge wholesale market is, so every conceivable item of food was there for sale. Michel had moved on, like me, and was now the managing director of the Windsor Hotel. We had pre-arranged to go through Paris, ending up on the outskirts, in Rungis, and would stop at the hotel with this very old fire engine on its way to the Beaujolais race, to give him some publicity. So we had a lunch party, with the French press, at his hotel, and then we went on our merry way down to Beaujolais.

John Dunn, the radio presenter was hilarious. He kept sending in reports to the BBC on how we were progressing and what happened, like the fact that no sooner had we left Michel Bontot's hotel, than it was pouring with rain, and the windscreen wipers suddenly failed to work. Well, if you've ever driven a lorry with pelting rain coming down at you with no windscreen wipers, you'd be a lucky chap to remain

alive. I can tell you, it's murder! I was a passenger at that time, and as
we went through the villages, to make sure we were on the right track
and could be seen or heard, I stuck my head out of the window and
rang the old fire bell. Well, everybody was totally astonished to see this
vehicle going through the villages. Anyway, we eventually managed
to get to Emile Chandesais' winery in good time, to everybody's utter
amazement. This old vehicle had taken ten days to get there, because we
were making a bit of a wine excursion en route. One of his engineers
repaired the wiper for us, so we were all set to leave on the race as soon
as the Beaujolais was released.

Before leaving at midnight, Emile put a dinner on for us, and we
all sat down in the wine cellars on bench seats at tables, with everybody
having lots of fun. At midnight, he opened the gate, and away we went.
Depending on your journey and how fast you went, you risked being
caught speeding by the police. If you were caught, you were fined and
disqualified; but as we were in our old vehicle, it didn't really matte
to us. We could barely reach thirty miles an hour in our hulking old
machine, so there was no chance of us speeding.

There was no way were we going to be anywhere near winning.
We returned to England, having had a pleasant journey back through
France, not arriving first, of course. We were, in actual fact, last—but it
didn't matter. The story was on the radio every day of our journey, and
when we got back, there were celebrations for the fact that we'd actually
made the whole journey at all, in this old vehicle. This old, chugging '42
fire engine made it home to much applause and publicity. A big lunch
was laid on, the Mayor of Liverpool came over, as much wine as could
be drunk was drunk, and everybody enjoyed the day. We drivers really
enjoyed the experience, even though it was relatively uncomfortable—
but you forget that when you're having fun.

Having now made this journey, I was hooked on the idea because
we'd got such good publicity. So, the following year, I managed to get
Renault to sponsor us and they gave us one of their latest Renault
Fuegos, their top marque sports car at the time.

It was the same routine as the year before: we were met by Emile and his son and we had the usual dinner and the usual midnight departure. However, this time around, we were not in a slow 1942 vehicle, we were in the latest, fastest sports car that Renault had produced, so we had it in our minds to win the race. And lo and behold, one of the hotels or restaurants had managed to obtain the great racing driver Sterling Moss to represent them as a contestant, so we were having to race against this most experienced Formula-1 driver. There were about 60 of us over from England, all in various cars or other types of transport, all out to make enough publicity in their own town to encourage people to eat at their restaurants and drink the Beaujolais nouveau.

Come midnight, the gates were opened and away went these 60 drivers. You can imagine what the atmosphere was like—if you think of Grand Prix racing, with everyone vying for a place to get away fastest. We had to judge when we could break the speed limit—which I honestly have to say, we did, once we'd got out of the area of the start, hoping that with so many people spreading out in all directions on so many different roads, the police wouldn't have set too many speed traps. Anyway, we got away with it. I think the French police somehow turned a blind eye on this weekend, because I went down there for about seven years and nobody seemed to get caught for speeding!

Anyway, I let the car go with some real zip, and we made our way to the ferry terminals. You had to decide in advance which port you were heading for, since they were in completely different directions, and we were driving towards that fork in the road. You either went left or right, depending on which of the ports you'd decided to depart from. I saw that Sterling Moss veered off to the left and I couldn't understand why he was doing this, but it was his decision. Perhaps he knew a shortcut to Calais.

I chose to go right, from Calais to Dover, and got there just minutes before the boat was about to sail, but at least I got my place. Not knowing what had happened, once we set sail, we walked through the ferry to see where Sterling Moss was, but to our great surprise, we couldn't find him. In fact, we were laughing our socks off, wondering where he'd got to.

"Perhaps he's waiting in the hold, revving up the car ready for the off!"

I eventually found out that he had chosen to go from Boulogne, a crossing which he thought was better suited to him, while we departed from Calais. However, he'd missed the boat, and had to wait another hour or two for the next ferry, while I was happily on my way. We had this enormous advantage on him, so we raced home as fast as we could and we won! Because of this bit of luck, we were able to say that we beat the famous racing driver Sterling Moss. We had an enormous amount of fun and a lot of press coverage again, being able to get the Beaujolais nouveau on the table before anybody else, so everybody was thrilled to bits.

Next year came along, and I really didn't know what to do. Then all of a sudden, somebody in the hotel mentioned an idea which piqued my interest: "Why don't you get one of these fast motorbikes to meet you in England and then tear up the motorway?"

Well, that's precisely what we did. We drove up in a car from Beaujolais to Dover as normal, then once we were in England, we rendezvoused with the biker, strapped the wine into his pannier baskets on the back of the motorbike, and I rode pillion home, with the wine. Well, I thought Blackpool Pleasure Beach had some scary rides, but this terrified me! The way he'd weave in and out at great speed, with this huge machine underneath him was petrifying, and it carried on all the way from Dover to Chester. I held on with white knuckles all the way, my grimace frozen in a rictus of fear. I've never been so thrilled and scared at the same time, as on the back of that motorbike. We won easily on that occasion, and yet again, we got our publicity. The press, as normal, gave us the best profile they could.

We did this for a few years, each time having to think how we would get better coverage from the press, because otherwise, it's stale news and they don't really want to know. A friend of mine in the meat trade had a Tiger Moth—the double-winged, single propeller plane, and he'd said he'd like to join in the fun. So that year, we landed in Dover, he took some cases of the latest vintage wine, and whilst we came up in the conventional way by car, he flew his Tiger Moth all the way back to Molly B at Chester and dropped a case of wine by parachute onto the lawn of the hotel. Well, this really caused hysterics, and gave us as much publicity as we'd ever had in any other race. We had achieved our desire, and we were getting rather well known for racing this wine home. Yet another daring win! I was getting notorious at winning these races because I used my imagination in selecting the most spectacular and effective kind of vehicle to use.

As time went by, we stopped racing. Eventually, the wine companies fell to the pressure of supermarkets and they let the big supermarkets have the wine earlier in the day instead of at midnight, so they got the wine onto the shelves in the supermarkets before we could possibly get it into our restaurants.

Sadly, the race gradually faded out because there was no point now in racing when the wine was already available in England. It lost its appeal and the whole thing collapsed. But they were years of tremendous fun, and it did cement great relationships within the wine trade. So that was a sideline: not really a holiday, but a period of having extra fun at work and good publicity for the hotel. So there you go— that's the story of the Beaujolais nouveau.

We're up to the end of 1987.

Olton Wade owned the big farm opposite the hotel, where they had Friesian milkers and a vast parlour. His was one of the most successful Cheshire cheese-making companies in the county. And with them being our neighbours, we all became extremely friendly. Olton used to work extremely hard in his spare time for the Conservative Party on the fundraising committee. Eventually, under Margaret Thatcher, he was knighted, and later entered the House of Lords.

One year, in '89, he came over and said that Margaret Thatcher was coming up, and would I like her to come to the hotel? Which opportunity, of course, I jumped at. He kept his promise and Margaret Thatcher came over, so we showed her around and she loved the hotel—to such an extent that a few months later I had a phone call to ask if the hotel could be vetted as a safe house for the Conservative Party. Not only for her own Ministers of State, but for visiting Ministers from abroad to stay in, because the way in which the hotel was built was ideal for the police security arrangements.

So we ended up with often getting phone calls from the Ministry of Defence or somewhere, asking for the Ministers to stay. In fact, the Northern Ireland Minister of State used to come over on a very regular basis, because we're not too far away from Northern Ireland. Because life over there was really quite severe, particularly during the ferocious battles with terrorists, his safety arrangements would sometimes get him down. So, without anybody knowing, I always used to open up the pool early in the morning, around six o'clock, so that he could come down on his own to relax, swim and use the facilities. He really enjoyed that.

Worshipful Company of Innholders

I will just give you a brief outline of the highest award that can be given to anyone within the hotel industry, which was bestowed upon me in 1992.

Henry VIII created what was known as the Worshipful Company of Innholders and developed an apprenticeship scheme for the benefit of young people in London. Really, it was designed to get them out of poverty by encouraging proper tradesmen to take these youngsters on as apprentices. The hostelry industry was made up of innholders, and the Worshipful Company of Innholders was created and prospered well. It had a chequered career, as did many of the worshipful companies, because all of their halls were in London and many of them were lost in the Great Fire. The Company of Innholders' Hall was one of those burned, and it wasn't until early Victorian times that the Innholders' Hall was rebuilt and the Innholders became active again. It had the one sole purpose of teaching young people, in the spirit in which it had first been created. The Worshipful Company of Master Innholders took into its membership one person per annum whom they believed had achieved the highest merits and done more for the industry than any other.

I was chosen to be a Master Innholder in '92.

I was proposed by Harry Murray at the five star Imperial Hotel in Torquay, and Herbert Strising, the managing director of The Savoy, who seemed to be my two sponsors. The candidates' list then went out to all the other members, and a vote was taken on who should be made a Master Innholder, subject to their passing the examination. You couldn't believe the excitement in my hotel, and even more so my home, when I was nominated for this wonderful position and honour! Let alone when I was offered it!

The day came when I had to go to London for the exam with the other candidates standing against me. Well, I hadn't been so nervous for many a year! The exam took place in the Innholders' Hall in the City of London, and we were shown into a room with a top table with nearly a dozen people seated at it, with one chair in the middle of the room for me to sit on. Well, if that's not daunting enough, I don't know what is! And of course, I was asked everything they could conceivably think of: what I had or had not done for the industry. I think one of the merits that gave me most points was the 20 years I'd spent involved with the college and the modern apprenticeship scheme I had set up. I think that really clinched it for me.

The examination went well, but they tried to trick me by asking, "What did you think of the statement made by the Ministry of Tourism at last night's dinner and speech?"

Well, luckily enough, I'd popped into The Savoy for a smoked salmon sandwich and a glass of Chardonnay because I felt I needed it before going down for the exam. Herbert had come up and was chatting to me about this very speech last night. So of course, I was able to answer the question with ease. Whether they agreed with what I said or not was immaterial; I was up-to date on recent thinking, I knew what had been said, and I had a view on it.

So eventually, after about two hours of interrogation, the exam finished and I left the hall in the City, breathing a sigh of relief. I went back to The Savoy and calmed down with another glass of Chardonnay.

I was later notified that I had become a member! I was expected to go down to the ceremony at The Guildhall in June, and I might bring my family down too, if I so wished.

So in June, I went down to The Guildhall with other Guilds taking on new members: in laundry or plumbing, the various trades. They all wore long gowns like university gowns, with ermine around the collars. We all went up and had to recite what we would do for the remaining part of our career, looking after apprentices and looking after The Mayor of London.

I came out of that ceremony as a Freeman of the City of London, too. To have been made a Master Innholder and a Freeman of the City of London made me one of the proudest persons you could imagine. I was so elated, and forever more, I was known in the higher echelons of the hotel industry for having reached this pinnacle. The one thing I had to continue to do, as stipulated, was to undergo continual training for the rest of my career to stay abreast of the latest developments within the industry. I thought that was a good idea, really, because it made you aware of industry innovations and there was no excuse to get out of it. I was also now able to put the letters IMA, MI after my name.

A short story, but one of great meaning in my life and of great meaning amongst other hoteliers.

I'm known as a Master Innholder and I try to attend whichever events I can, and keep in touch with all the members and my contemporaries within the industry, especially still being a director of Smith Hotel at Gretna Green.

The arrival of the KGB

So, life went on, with us suddenly getting these telephone calls to accommodate politicians, and then one day I got a phone call from the Prime Minister's Secretary, wanting to arrange for the second most powerful politician in Russia to come and stay for the week.

". . . Would that be in order?" he asked.

It would, indeed!

With his own entourage and the KGB, he would like to visit as many independent British companies as he could, to learn how free enterprise worked within our country, to compare it with how things operated in their communist system. So, all the arrangements were made and the security scrutiny was ramped up to a higher degree: our accounts, registers of future and past residents of the hotel, and all of the staff were screened even more rigorously than normal. But, of course, there were no problems at all. The only way we managed to keep looking after all these dignitaries was because the loyalty of my staff meant that they never revealed that important people were coming to the hotel—for which I give them tremendous credit, because it would be so easy for one of them to slip a note to a reporter, stating that such people were going to be here.

So, the day came when Mr Khasbulatov, the Russian Prime Minister, arrived. Of course, he arrived very discreetly indeed in this huge Russian car—with an ostentatious escort of numerous police outriders and KGB security guards. It really caused such a palaver—it was unbelievable, all for the safety of this very important man!

I greeted him, and he was most courteous and glad to be here.

"In fact, Mr Mawdsley, I would like your help with my mission!" he said.

I nodded, always pleased to assist, whilst wondering how, exactly, I could help a powerful Russian politician—with his mission.

"I would like help to meet many of the most . . . how you say?" he turned to his interpreter and barked a Russian word.

"Influential," the interpreter said calmly.

". . . Influential . . ." repeated Khasbulatov, " . . . businessmen of large and small companies in your region."

"Yes, indeed," I agreed. "We can invite them here."

"Da. I will have dinner party of about 25 people, every night."

"Yes, I would be delighted to arrange that," I said, my mind whirling with possibilities.

"Except Saturday," he smiled. "Saturday, I rest!" he chuckled and continued, "But I insist you join me also to dine on each night."

All the arrangements were made swiftly and smoothly, and I was delighted to be invited to join the guests at the table. Until the first night.

I was just chatting to the entrepreneur seated next to me before the first course was served, when Khasbulatov rapped a knife on a wine glass to draw everyone's attention. The room fell silent and he paused, smiling, before he announced, "I would like to have dinner in the Russian custom, whereby I, as host, will choose somebody in the room to make a speech of his own liking during the meal."

I got the shock of my life. I was seated opposite him at the other end of the table, and throughout the starter, I kept seeing him sort of eyeing me up. I thought, "Oh, goodness gracious me!" I just had an inner knowing that he was going to ask me to be the first person to do this, and of course, my instinct was right.

He suddenly raised his hand and asked for quiet in the room, before he said, "In accordance with the Russian custom, I would like to ask Mr Mawdsley to make the first speech!"

So I had to make a speech, totally off the cuff. Of course, I chose my own subject and made it as appropriate to the occasion as I could: *how tourism could help the negotiations and peace between our countries*. It's just as well that I am unfazed by public speaking and passionate about my vocation. It went down extremely well, and to my relief, at least it was out of the way! I could relax for the rest of the meal, and during all the other evenings!

In between each course, Khasbulatov would call again for hush and we would have a toast to somebody or something, and down would go a generous glass of vodka. And the vodka was not the mild 40% proof sort we are used to here; he'd brought along this powerful Russian vodka with him, so, by the end of the evening, after many enthusiastic toasts and many explosively strong vodkas, we non-Russians were in quite a state, whilst the Russians were not affected at all.

At all times, Khasbulatov had his pack of serious-faced KGB guards in the room, close by, which evidently irked him. He was most cynical about them and snappily told them to be quiet when they muttered in the background; it was obvious that he hated them.

This ritual process went on every evening, until the last dinner occurred on Friday night, and after his day of rest, Khasbulatov was leaving on Sunday morning. I met him in the hall on Saturday morning and was chatting away to him, when I asked, "Have you ever been into an English home?"

He said wryly, "No, I haven't. But I would love to."

Suddenly I said, on impulse, "Well, would you like to come to dinner at my home?"

"Yes, I would love to," he said, "but without the KGB. The scoundrels. It is a private party, after all, and not a state visit. I don't need those idiots there. I have to bring my personal bodyguard, though, and I would like to bring the French attaché."

That was all fine with me, and by the time we had finished discussing who should attend, the party ended up as about a dozen people. I picked up the telephone to ring Gaby at home, and told her, "I've just done something you might not be terribly happy about."

"What?" she asked, with trepidation, although she knew me by now, and could often expect the unexpected.

"Um. I don't know how we're going to cope, but I've invited the Russian Prime Minister for dinner at home tonight. Oh. And the French attaché. And . . . about ten other people . . ."

Well, poor Gaby almost collapsed!

I said hurriedly, "I'll come home in a minute and we'll talk it through, but the Russian said yes, he wants to come."

So, I went home and we discussed how best we could manage this, especially since we weren't able to speak any Russian. We would have to use the interpreter or the French attaché who could speak Russian to our visitors, so that all worked out. We discussed the menu with the chef and planned to have rack of lamb, which the chef would cook in the kitchens and bring over to the house.

So, that was all fine and I went to collect Khasbulatov at six o'clock. The hotel staff told me that we had three weddings on in the hotel that day—which was normal, because we were so popular—two small ones and the big one in the ballroom. Well, unbeknown to us, Mr Khasbulatov had been walking in the gardens when he'd decided to join the queue for the biggest wedding reception. And of course, when he came to shake the hands of the bride and groom, it came out that the Russian Prime Minister wanted to attend an English wedding reception. They graciously asked him to join them. There can't be that many weddings that are gatecrashed by a top Russian politician! I'm sure it stayed in the happy couple's memory as much as it did ours!

So, by the time I came to collect him to come home to dine with us, he'd been celebrating the couple's happy day, doubtlessly with numerous toasts—both English and Russian—and had already had a fair amount to drink. When we arrived back home, most of our party was in the lounge where everybody already had their drinks, so I asked Mr Khasbulatov what he would like.

"Some white wine," he slurred, so I went into the kitchen and brought a bottle of wine out—a rather nice bottle of Chardonnay—poured him a glass and placed the bottle on the dining room table, ready for our meal. He was so relieved that he was no longer being watched by the hated KGB that he was very relaxed and at home, and his generous consumption of alcohol had put him in a rather good mood.

The early part of the evening progressed very beautifully, with us all chatting over drinks, and exchanging pleasant small-talk, when suddenly someone cried, "Where is Mr Khasbulatov?"

We all looked at one another. Somehow, he wasn't with us. We momentarily panicked, but quickly discovered that he was in the garden. That was fine—as everybody knows, I've got a rather nice garden and he had been wandering around at his leisure, looking at what we had planted in there and enjoying the soft evening sunshine. However, he had taken the bottle of wine along with him, and by this time, he had consumed the entire bottle. And that, together with his previous all-day drinking, had suddenly caused him to collapse into a crumpled Russian heap, still holding tightly onto the empty wine bottle.

Well, honestly, if you put yourself in my shoes: the Russian Prime Minister collapsed drunk in my garden, you'd die, like I nearly did. Happily enough, my house adjoins the hotel, so his personal bodyguard and one of the staff hauled him up by the armpits and frog-marched him through the gardens and into the hotel the back way (since discretion is, of course, paramount), and up to his room, where they put him to bed. So that somewhat calmed us, but it was very alarming, as you can well imagine.

At midnight, having regained consciousness and a raging appetite, Khasbulatov telephoned for room service and said that he would now like to have the rack of lamb that he'd missed having in my home. I gritted my teeth, thinking, "Here we go again!"

I was contemplating further toasts and speeches and wine and vodka in a sort of nocturnal groundhog day. But the Russian Prime Minister had 'the munchies'. What can one do?

We had to go and wake the chef up, get him to come into the hotel, cook the required meal for Khasbulatov, and the Russian Premier was served the meal as room service. After which he went to sleep, thank goodness. And on Sunday morning all the official cars came and collected him, all the goodbyes were said, and off he went. We gave a big sigh of relief, as did all the staff, after that week that nobody will ever forget, Gaby and I least of all.

When Khasbulatov returned to Russia, we received a lovely letter from him inviting us to Russia as his guests, which enamoured us. And he sent a traditional country craft set of goblets made of wood, gilded with gold. What a lovely thought and present we'd received for our endeavours! At that time, Yeltsin was the president of Russia, and there were some differences of opinion between Mr Khasbulatov as Acting Chairman of the Presidium of the Supreme Soviet, and Mr Yeltsin. This disagreement mounted into something horrendous, and the clash of egos between Khasbulatov and Yeltsin led to the Russian constitutional crisis of 1993, in which Khasbulatov led the Russian Supreme Soviet against the president, which ended with Yeltsin's violent assault on parliament. The armed forces were called in, the Russian Houses of Parliament were bombed and Khasbulatov was arrested along with other leaders of parliament, before its dissolution in October 1993. It went down in history, and of course, we never got our lovely visit as his guests, because he was now in isolation.

These are the sort of things that happened to us.

Olton Wade had been asked to show the Queen round his dairy plant, so she came up and we had the pleasure of seeing her, too. And a couple of years later, after Margaret Thatcher had been ousted from the Conservative Party and John Major was Prime Minister, we received a request from Downing Street asking if John Major could spend the Bank Holiday weekend with us. Once again, the security arrangements were activated, but we'd got used to all this by now and took no notice of them. But the odd thing was that he was travelling by car and coming through Wales, so he was escorted by the Welsh Police until he crossed the border, then security was transferred to English command. The week before his arrival, we were given the private telephone numbers of his personal secretary and staff in London, should we need to make contact with anybody. We didn't worry, however.

Everything went fine, except that by ten o'clock in the morning on the Bank Holiday Friday, most of the car park was cleared of all cars, but there was one man still sitting in his car, just a few yards away, on the other side of the car park, far from the front door. I was tipped off by staff that this man was there, and we all grew a bit concerned because he was just sitting there for ages, and didn't seem to want to leave the car. I warned people not to approach him, since we didn't know whether he might be dangerous, or his car booby-trapped.

So here's where things went wrong. I rang the private numbers I'd been given, in some concern, since I thought I'd better warn the Prime Minister's security team, and you would hardly credit it, but as sure as I'm sitting here today, none of the lines were answered. People were off making arrangements and weren't answering their telephones. My next idea was to ring the Chester Police headquarters, but because I couldn't say who it concerned or what it was about, I was given short shrift.

"All I can say is," I told them, "It is of a most serious nature and I need to speak to the Chief Constable of Chester to give me some assistance."

Well, either they thought I was a lunatic or he was unavailable, but I got nowhere with Chester headquarters because I wasn't allowed to say who we were expecting. It was all being taken care of by government security, the way they normally looked after dignitaries. But because a mixture of Welsh and English police were involved, somehow it all seemed to be a bit tangled and complicated.

So I said to myself, "Well, bloody hell, I'm in such a mess, now. I don't know what this man is. Is he armed? And I can't get any help."

I was desperate by now, with the Prime Minister shortly to arrive and an armed assassin sitting in our car park. I went round to the local bobby's house in the village and told him we suspected that there was a man wishing to do the Prime Minister some harm, and the police officer was in a quandary about what to do, too. He was used to taking reports of lost bikes and dealing with occasional happy drunks wearing traffic cones on their heads; he was not used to apprehending trained killers. He came round to my house and we tried to work out how we could confront this man without getting murdered for our pains. The man seemed to have no back-up of his own, but in the end, our bobby decided that he'd better just call the local police and of course, they responded to his request for assistance.

The Prime Minister was due at any moment, and to our amazement and concern, the suspicious-looking man decided to choose that moment to drive out of our car park just as the Prime Minister was driving in. Well, by this time the police had suddenly woken up to give chase and their sirens were blaring all around. I'm sure John Major wondered what the hell was going on!

The man was eventually stopped further up the road by this contingent of police cars. It turned out that he was a private investigator trying to determine whether or not the wife of his client had a boyfriend with her in the hotel. He was taken away for questioning, while we had to resume the calm attitude of greeting the Prime Minister and taking him to his suite. Next, there was such a hoo-ha again, because nobody could find Mrs Major's luggage! So our calm suddenly turned again into the panicked cries of: "Where's Mrs Major's luggage gone?"

It turned out that Mrs Major had not even come, let alone her luggage. John Major was meeting Bertie Ahern, the Irish Prime Minister, to start finding a way to break the deadlock and begin peace talks with Northern Ireland. So, of course, I'll never forget the whole episode.

John Major wrote me a lovely, long letter, signed and handwritten to me personally, and about two days later I had a chuckle, because an official letter came up from Downing Street, thanking me and the staff for what we had done. And I thought, well, John Major wrote to me personally, long before his office had bothered. Then he sent me a ministry cricket bat, signed with thanks, because he was a great cricket supporter. And that was the end of that episode.

So, you can see now how our standing within the hotel industry built up over the first few years and became so well established.

The next three to four years really passed without any incident. The company was very solid, all the hotels were running exceptionally well, the management structure was right, and I wasn't sure where we were going or what I was going to do next. As it happened, in November 1995 I went to London for the International Hotel Conference, which is a sales workshop—a trade show, in other words. Every hotel or organization in the hospitality industry would buy a stand at Earl's Court, which has a huge number of rooms designed especially for this sort of work, and you take a stand as big as you want for the size of your company. Well, I was chatting away to prospective buyers of holiday products, because that's what it was all about, getting as much business as you could out of it.

A gentleman by the name of Robert Breare met me and was just chatting, wanting to know more about my company, and of course I told him. And then during 1996, Robert approached me to see whether I would sell the company to Arcadian Hotels, which is a small company of deluxe hotels. This gave me a shock. I'd had many approaches over the years to sell our hotel and I just didn't even have to think about it, casually saying no on every previous occasion; but somehow, his approach made me actually think about it.

So, in December 1996, during the Christmas holidays, Gaby and I had a long discussion with the Walker family and the Board. Angelique was already qualified as a vet and had no desire whatsoever to be involved in the hotel, and Christine was on her way in the financial world of the hotel industry, where she could work from nine to five and hopefully enjoy a family. We were getting older, all our money was tied up in bricks, and it wasn't as if I could go and spend £20,000's worth of bricks on buying a yacht; our money was locked up.

We met Robert Breare again and started to negotiate, seeing what he wanted to do to the hotel, how he would look after the staff, and what assurances he would give us that his word was his bond, because I'd seen so many deals done that were broken the next day. Anyway, it all came down to it eventually, after very hard bargaining, because Gaby didn't want to sell Solberge, the hotel we had up in Yorkshire; she wanted to keep it. It was small, it did so well and she loved it so much. Whereas Mollington was a huge machine with now over 100 rooms and a leisure club: a big operation, Solberge's clientele and the way in which it operated was so different. But I failed to negotiate its exclusion—Robert wanted the company as a whole. And in the end, we sold.

For the first time in my life, I was very rich. I felt very guilty about the staff who had worked for me, some of them having started the day I arrived, and very, very many of them having worked for me for 20 years or more. They were part of our family; they'd helped bring up the children, and it was a close family business—but I had to let go of it, and of them. So it hurt a bit, really.

But time heals these things, and Gaby and I got a bit bored. We found that we didn't like the idea of the hotel next door no longer belonging to us, so we disappeared to the States for three months—another holiday. Then, on our return, things had calmed down.

I refused to go back into the hotel, although we'd been given life membership of the club, but I never set foot in it. Gaby does; Gaby still goes swimming now, but I don't.

So that was the end of 32 years of the Molly B.

The Gambler and Accident

I'm not really sure how I'm going to get on with the story of my accident. It's not really something I want to speak of, but I suppose that readers should know; as painful as it is to me. However, I'm quietly sitting here in the lounge and at the moment I am fairly composed. I can begin.

You know that I had a passion for hunting. Being the personality that I was, I adored hunting up at the front with the huntsman; I was Secretary to the Cheshire Forest Hunt, and I've hunted with them for just over 30 years. My best horse, The Gambler, hunted with me for 14 years and he was almost human in understanding your moods and instinctively knowing what you wanted from him. He was well known amongst the Forest as one of the finest hunters around. Unfortunately, after 14 years of faithful service, The Gambler broke his knee. That, as you can well imagine, like the loss of any pet, broke my heart.

Together with the family, however, a very good friend, Mark Chambers, the dealer I bought all my horses from, persuaded me not to give up because I adored being out; not only hunting, but with my own family. We'd been out throughout every year since the children were ten, spending the days hunting and especially enjoying the journeys to the hunt in the lorry, which always seemed to be the place for ironing out their problems. And then, once on our horses, all was fresh and new—our troubles forgotten—it was another day.

I eventually bought from Mark a lovely Irish young horse who was a five year old, and everybody said, "You silly old man. You want an eight year old!"

We were in the pub and I asked a very experienced rider, well known in the eventing field, "Laura, do you know where I can have this young horse trained?"

She said, "Yes, I do know someone in your area. Her name is Louise Lyons and she's actually in the pub now, if you're interested."

She introduced me to her and since I didn't really know much about her or her background, or even how good she was, I simply asked her if she was capable of bringing on a young horse.

She turned round to me as bold as brass and said, "John, I am bloody good. Not good—bloody good!"

So I said, "Well, on that basis, will you take my horse in livery, and school him?"

Which she did, with some skill. We entered into some light eventing during the summer months, and I got to know Mr Chips. Not quite as well as The Gambler, but nevertheless, we got on well.

On 5th November 2005, a Wednesday, we had been hunting for a while at Lord Darlesbury's estate near here. It's renowned for its hunting and hedges—he kept them in good order and well cut. On a Wednesday it's quieter, and the field—the number of people out—was not great, so you could take what is known as 'your own line', which means you could go anywhere you wished to jump. We were cantering on at quite some speed and a hedge was in front of us. It was in full view, and I was totally confident, so we took the jump. Unfortunately, the horse had jumped so high that I was jumped off, as it's known in hunting terms. I'm told I landed on my neck.

I don't remember any more.

I was rushed to hospital immediately. For a while, my life hung in the balance. I wasn't conscious, and wasn't able to breathe for myself. At one stage, Gaby and the family were called at two in the morning, and asked to come in, believing that I was not going to live much longer. However, I did. Then I lay there in limbo in the isolation ward for two weeks. In order for them to save my life, they had to operate, and inserted a tracheotomy, which is a hole in the throat into which a trachea unit is inserted to allow you to breathe.

Eventually, two weeks later, I gradually seemed to come round and found myself in Warrington Hospital in the intensive care unit, on a ventilator 24 hours a day. I could not speak, due to the accident having snapped the spinal cord of my neck, affecting my vocal cords. So, whenever Gaby came—which, bless her cotton socks, was every day—the only way we could communicate was by Gaby showing me the letters of the alphabet on a card, like in an optician's. She would point to them, I would nod and she would write the letter down until we made a word. Painstakingly, we would continue writing the words until she could either guess what the sentence was, or the sentence was completed. This was the only way we could communicate. For me, apart from having lost the movement of all my limbs and feeling below the middle of my chest, not being able to talk was almost the final straw. But I really couldn't do much about it and the hospital said they hoped that, in time, my voice would come back.

I remained in Warrington Hospital while they tried to stabilise me. They had a funny system, having four consultants who worked on a duty rota list, each one taking over from another. You never really knew which consultant was yours or where you were up to with them, or who was taking responsibility for you. The whole affair appeared to me to be totally disorganised.

They made contact with the two spinal hospitals within my region: Gobowen, which is famous for spinal units, and Southport. We chose to Gobowen as we were familiar with it from previous occasions and knew Professor Eisenstein very well indeed. However, they didn't have a ventilator system there, so I had to go to Southport, the only difficulty being that they had no beds at that moment. It was only a small self-contained unit, of 48 beds, run by Mr Sett and Mr Salmi quite autonomously from the rest of the hospital in almost every way. But at this stage, I couldn't even get in there.

Well, I spent four months in this hospital and I can't tell you how much I disliked it. There was no real care from any doctor or staff to help you get along. I still couldn't seem to get a bed in Southport and I was getting nowhere in Warrington. I could not see a way forward, or even a glimpse of my life improving. I was really in a very low state physically, and even more so mentally, because I had no goals to go forward with. During the night of April 2nd, '06, I decided that life was not worth living and my best option was to terminate it. I just had to decide how I was going to achieve this objective, given that I was almost completely immobile—only being able to move my head—and couldn't even speak. I thought it would be better for me, better for Gaby and the whole family, because I'd lived a very lovely, happy 70 years up to then, and just wanted to let it come to an end.

However, something happened. I must have been heard somehow, somewhere, but on the afternoon of the third of April, Dr John Watts from Southport Hospital came to see me. He was shocked to see the condition I was in and promised me that he would get me a bed as fast as possible in Southport Spinal Unit. So, finally I'd got a goal. I dismissed the previous night's thoughts altogether and awaited John's promise.

The hospital was instructed by the Southport Spinal Unit in how to wean me off the ventilator. However, they were unsuccessful insofar as they were too dogmatic. But at last, the day came when, happily, I was moving to the Spinal Unit at Southport, and I went straight into the Intensive Care Unit under the person we all called "Matron". All the Unit's nursing staff were shared between the intensive care and highly dependent patients, so there was an enormous degree of continuity of nursing staff, and they really cared and looked after the patients like nurses only dreamed of.

Adapting

I spent a year in this ward, and so I knew and was known by everybody. We had four other patients—one I disliked immensely, and the others I got on well with. I can't say that this initial miracle of moving me had too much effect after the first few weeks. However, I was assigned to Mr Salmi, the senior consultant of the hospital, as my personal consultant, and he came to see me every day of the week except for Saturday, when he took a day off. I had Dr John Watts, who was my respiratory consultant, and a young lady called Sue Perry-Davis, who had a boy and a girl of 12 years old and a very, very happy family. It turned out that Sue was going to be the person responsible for looking after me on an ongoing basis and ensuring that I made progress.

I really can't describe how I could possibly take in the differences before and after the accident. It took weeks and months, I think, to face the horror of having lost the use of everything I'd had, and to accept being incapable of doing everything I was so used to doing, even unconsciously—like breathing. At this stage, I could no longer move or speak, and I was still on the ventilator 24 hours a day. But I had the encouragement of the whole team there, and my wife who visited me five days a week if she could, sometimes with her friends driving to save her the stress of it. Otherwise, there I was, paralysed, not knowing what was going to happen.

Well, first of all, Sue came to me and said, "John, we need a plan of how we are going to improve your life. The first steps are to gradually get you off the ventilator and off the drip-feed, and into a state where you can breathe for short amounts of time each day."

And she really, really did mean 'short'—we're talking just minutes at this stage, because after one minute of trying to breathe, I was desperate to get back onto the ventilator, at first. It was purely through Sue's and Matron's patience and determination that I did what they wanted, and Sue had a happy knack of blending both infinite patience and steely determination. Some days, I would just have to get on with it and do as I was told, and on other days Sue would relax and let me go back onto the ventilator within a shorter time than was really allowed.

This programme took months, but eventually the stage came when I no longer had to rely on Gaby's alphabet card, because I could actually speak a whole sentence and for short times, somehow, we could talk. My breathing without the machine grew to something like two hours, and I was able to come off the drip-feed. So from a doctor's point of view, physically, I was improving.

Mentally, I could not come to terms with the thought of having to be as I was, with no positive chance of any substantial improvement, and the constant humiliation of having to rely on others for everything. Always having to ask for help from someone to do things for me was terrible.

But things slowly improved, and Mr Salmi decided to take a risk and referred me to the occupational therapist. By this time, I was now off the ventilator for a few hours in the morning, so I would go downstairs to the occupational therapists' unit and attempt simple tasks, like trying to roll a ball or make my hands move or get some part of my body to react. Everybody was hopeful that at least some part of my upper body would respond. However, I'm sorry to say, nothing did. So that was yet another disappointment in the progress of my recovery programme.

But Sue's hard work in enabling me to stay off the ventilator more and more, and her and John's teaching me how to speak again gave me some flutters of hope.

My time at the occupational therapist was extended to working with a lady called Dorothy, who came into that department on a completely voluntary basis, to teach patients how to operate a computer. At first we tried a system of blowing and sucking a mouthpiece to activate the keys on the computer. For some reason, I couldn't make this work to my satisfaction.

But one day, Mr Salmi was in the room while I was unsuccessfully blowing the damn thing in frustration, and he said, "Why don't we try and get John to make the computer work by attaching a golf ball to the end of the apparatus of the computer system?"

Well, we got quite a shock: I actually did manage to make it work somewhat. However, it wasn't as comfortable as I would have wished, so using their ingenuity we decided to use a tennis ball, and between that and the strength now in my voice, voice recognition software was added to my computer and I could actually get the computer to operate.

Progress was being made on all fronts, really. Dorothy had managed to enable me to talk to or dictate onto the computer instead of typing, I was able to go onto the internet like anybody else, and my voice was strengthening. So, all in all, I'd reached the stage when Mr Salmi decided that I could come out of the Intensive Care Unit and go into High Dependency. It didn't make much difference to me, really, since the staff intermingled between the two units so I had the same staff and the same consultants as before. There was just a different set of patients within the room.

Dr Clive was deputy to Mr Salmi running the Unit, but was also a qualified psychiatrist. He kept coming to see me to help me get over the remaining problems I had, since I had not yet come to terms with being in a wheelchair. I realise now that these chaps are quite clever, because they work in such a fashion that you don't realise exactly what is happening, until you look back and realize that you've improved:

that things are not so bad, and you can actually find some meaning in life and feel better. But slowly, I suppose my character was beginning to come through again; I was beginning to combat this fear and look forward to each day as it came, and Gaby's continuous support in coming so often gave me sustenance. We were now able to put the ventilator and suction machine onto the back of my chair and go downstairs to the garden and duck pond—yet another step forward. I got outside for the first time in months, and it felt like the first time in my life I'd felt the breeze on my face, seen the blue sky and greenness of the grass, and listened to birdsong. I felt alive again.

At this stage, I was in an ordinary hospital wheelchair but I began to wish I had an electric one because Gaby's back is not in the best of health, and trying to push me really was not very good for her.

And lo and behold, Jean Webb, through the Master Innholders and the BHA (the British Hoteliers Association), organised a fund to buy me the most up-to-date electric chair on the market. Well, can you imagine how I felt? That all these colleagues had donated money and bought me this highly sophisticated electric chair which cost the price of a new car! I jumped for joy when it arrived, because it really did live up to expectations, and my tennis ball adaptation allowed me to drive myself wherever I wanted. Well, there we go—another step.

Fighting for home

I'd now been in the hospital at Southport for 18 months, and the team could see that I was improving and becoming stable enough, both physically and mentally, until there was a real possibility of me returning home. Well, if you think that I'd already spent close on two years in hospitals, the idea of going to my own home was the best gift of all.

In due course, my case for release was put to the PCT, the National Health Primary Care Trust, and I waited quite a while for their decision because they don't move very fast at the best of times. Eventually, I was told that they refused to let me go home. They said this would not be possible and that I would have to be looked after in a care home for now. They'd found one at the Countess of Chester Hospital, just down the road from me, and they decided to take me down there one day to show me around. Well, after we'd visited it, although it was very nice and appeared to be very well run, it was a far cry from having my own independence, my own home, my own freedom and being with my family again.

At the time, I was a Director of Blackpool Pleasure Beach, I had my own consultancy business, and I had successfully built Geoffrey

Thompson, the MD of Blackpool Pleasure Beach, a fabulous hotel of unique conception within the hotel industry. I wasn't ready for a care home.

My brother, Richard, had come up to the hospital every single Thursday without fail all the time I was in both hospitals, he rang Gaby every single night and had dealt with any difficulties that had arisen in my business. Richard was actually in the hospital when I was told I had to go into a home, and knowing my wishes, we tried to find a way of disputing this.

Life has some ironic twists and turns, because Richard went home, and over the weekend he was in the garden and got talking to his neighbours, which he hadn't really done during all the time he'd lived there. By some miracle, the lady of the house was a solicitor, mainly retained by the PCT to act for them in cases of dispute! So, Richard, without mentioning anything about me, casually asked her in a friendly manner, "So, which solicitor do you fear most? You know, who do you dislike going up against in court?"

Well, she turned round to Richard quite openly and said, "Oh— that would be Yogi Yamin. He works for McKinley's in Sheffield. He's frighteningly good."

So, armed with this information, Richard came up the next week and we telephoned Yogi from the hospital to see what the chances were of him acting for me and taking on my case for the family. He said straight out, "I only take twenty percent of the cases put before me, so don't take it personally if I say no."

Fortunately, after hearing what had happened and the boat I was in, he agreed in principle to take my case on. He then carefully went through the costs involved up until the day we went into court, which were fine by us. And then he said, "But if we have to go to court, I'm afraid to say that the fees jump quite dramatically, and if you lose the case you will have to pay all the costs of the PCT and their advocates."

Well, I practically needed the ventilator again! This didn't half put a brake on things, since the costs would be enormous! However, he did say, "I recently won three big cases and I'm well known now for winning the cases I fight."

So, Gaby and I, and the family at home talked. The dreadful thought of me being forced into residential care and having no freedom horrified me. The family agreed with me. So I said to Yogi, "No matter what happens, please take the case on."

Well, this took some time, as the legal profession doesn't work at high speed, and I was almost ready to be discharged from hospital by then. The PCT stuck to their guns, and wouldn't change their decision.

Yogi said, "If that's the case, we are going to court."

So the worst scenario had come to bear and we braced ourselves for the massive cost. I'd decided that I would have to sell quite a few shares and use our savings to pay for Yogi to represent me in court. It wasn't just a matter of principle, since the reality was that my independence had already been taken away to devastating effect, and now the PCT wanted to curtail my choices further. I just wanted to go home.

The day before the hearing, Yogi received a phone call to say that the PCT had withdrawn the case. You don't know how wonderful that was—the whole family was jubilant, and champagne was drunk by many people, including the staff, knowing that yet another fight had been won. I was going to have my own freedom, my own care, forever—and paid for by the PCT.

I was, in due course, coming home. I progressed in hospital on my various machines while Social Services met Gaby to discuss the transformation of the house. Then the builder was called in, and work started.

The ground floor of our spare day room and conservatory had been transformed into accommodation for me, and I have to say, it did look beautiful. We had a team of carers who were going to look after me, and I started to try to settle into my home.

But the ecstatic moments were soon dispelled. Neither of us, especially Gaby, had been advised about how radically our personal lives would be infringed upon. We had not been advised to build a staff room, which really was the biggest error, because the care staff seemed to be everywhere, particularly for Gaby. The woman of the house likes her own kitchen and it was being continually used on my behalf by my staff, and this caused a lot of friction, really, which was a bit unsettling for us all. I asked Gaby to be home, but Gaby found it very difficult to accept all this change. I don't know all of her feelings on this; I only know, as a husband knows instinctively, how she felt.

Furthermore, now that I was at home, the reality of my disabilities truly sank in for me. In hospital, you get used to a daily routine and you have a hospital life amongst other people. 'Institutionalised' might be one word for it. You are occupied by occupational therapists, gym and all sorts of activities, so you don't really think too much about how it's going to be in the outside world. Funnily enough, it felt a little like I'd been a prisoner who'd longed to be let out, but is at a loss when it finally happens. I couldn't do anything for myself in any way, except talk, and ask for assistance. Everywhere I went, there was always somebody with me, except in the garden where I was at least able to control my wheelchair with my own driving attachment, if you remember.

I had lost my old life along with my independence—and with it went my sense of identity and purpose. This really played on my mind and got me down rather a lot. I had to relearn all over again and prepare myself for another chapter of life. I had fought through using my willpower, but had been helped in particular by the team at the hospital—especially Sue, and I missed them dreadfully. It took a long time for me to start to want to telephone people, or talk to people outside the house. My brother, Richard, bless his cotton socks, still came up to see me and telephoned daily. I had to sit down and think carefully—and really decide that I had to get out of this negative frame of mind and pull myself together. So, with the help of Gaby, more than anybody, I started to try and think of things to do.

When we'd sold the hotel back in '95/'96, I had been bored and took my degree in portrait photography. Now everybody, particularly Gaby and my family, said, "Well, John, *there's* a project for you."

I had thousands and thousands of negatives, and David, one of my carers, was interested in working with me on this project—even though it seemed that it was going to take forever. But it didn't matter, really, because it was something that occupied my mind and gave me something positive to do. The idea was that I was going to compile a book out of the photographs that I'd sort out.

Except one day, Mike, a computer wizard who was my age with his own business, Bytecraft Limited, said, "For goodness sake, John! Why do you want to make a book when you've got the world at your fingertips? Why don't we put the photos onto your own website? I will help you design the website for a nominal charge."

So, nearly every day, David and I went through these negatives and gradually picked out the ones I thought were technically good enough and hopefully of sufficient merit for people to want to look at. This was one of the projects I set up, but I still had to get myself out of the house.

I don't know what it was, but I really did *not* want to know anything about the horse, and nobody could change my mind.

But slowly we began to go out shopping, or to the cinema, or to the afternoon theatre performance at the Lowry in Manchester, which is the theatre we most love. Although the pain I had to tolerate was still there and got worse as we travelled more, I began to enjoy getting out in the world, and this progressed onto me meeting up with some of my friends from the past. My email was workable, so I was able to write to friends and get a response.

I don't know what it was, but a cloud still seemed to be hanging over me. I think it was the horses. There was a great part of my life missing, but one that was unbearable for me to think about. I was, if I'm honest, afraid to go to a hunt again.

Binnie, a carer who had been with me since the very beginning, decided one Saturday morning to take me to the hunt at Paul Hogarth's. I was both terrified and excited, but agreed to go. It was the most popular meet in the Forest calendar, only because of Paul's enormous hospitality. So, all in one go, I met all of the foot followers and mounted members of the hunt again, and I quite enjoyed it. I'd got over my reluctance now, and managed at least to meet my old hunting set. I would say that perhaps half my friends are in the hunting or riding worlds, so I had missed out on a lot.

Then they encouraged me to go to Lord Ashcroft's meet at Arley. He is slightly older than me, and when I arrived there, his eyebrows shot up in shock at the sight of me. He exclaimed, "Good God, John—I can't believe you're in a wheelchair and not on your horse!"

He made such a fuss of me to make me feel welcome, ensuring that I was comfortable, with a drink and food and a good view of the proceedings. This had two effects: I felt privileged to be welcomed so warmly, but I was also dreadfully upset. I struggled to maintain my composure, my throat tightening with a lump of sadness and despair threatening to bubble up.

"Bye, Daddy!" Angelique waved to me from horseback and rode off, and that was the last straw. I finally broke down in tears, sobs racking my body, and I couldn't stop crying.

Gaby leant over me in great concern.

"Please—take me away!" I sobbed. Embarrassed as well as distraught, I needed to get away to calm down. "Take me home!"

This upset me for quite some time. However, I thought it through, summoned my willpower, and said to myself, "Well, I know I'm like this now, and I'm not going to change. I like the people and I like the horses. I will just have to come to terms with the situation and enjoy what I can."

And I gradually did. I went to one or two more meets and eventually I began to lose the fear, so it became a joy again.

Sadly, one day Angelique's horse had a breathing problem and they had to perform a very rare operation, in the theatre at Leahurst. Via webcam, they managed to talk to an American veterinary surgeon who had performed the operation, and between them they tried to repair the damage. Things weren't going well, and the only man to help was in Newmarket but he said clearly on the telephone that he doubted even he could save the horse. So sadly, they had to let him go. Both Angie and Christine had ridden this horse since the day they'd started hunting, some 14 or 15 years previously, and in all that time each of them had only come off once. You become so attached to a pet, and the bond you have with a horse is very special, so it upset everybody, as you can imagine.

I was great friends with a girl called Louise Lyons, who looked after our horses up on the Wirral, and I asked Louise to see if she could find something else.

Not too long afterwards, she called me to the yard, where she had a silver-grey stallion tied up waiting for me. She'd bought this horse about three years ago as an unknown and personally trained him to this stage. She believed that he was quite capable of looking after the girls and doing more than he had been asked to do. He was very expensive, but I trusted her, as I always had done in the past, so I helped buy the horse for them, and for me to enjoy the eventing season in the summer.

Well, we all got our rewards. He turned out to be a brilliant hunter, and for our first season we gained three rosettes. Ironically, the most difficult event of the season for his grade was Arley, where he came third.

So, I'd now won the battle of the horse, and everybody just accepted seeing me around in my wheelchair, whether it was across the field or in someone's yard. The chair went wherever I wanted, just as I was promised when we bought it.

When I came home, unknown to me, the hunt had decided to collect a fund to allow me to have the most up-to-date television/DVD player and the latest laptop computer system for all my projects. Well, it just shows you, no matter what field you're in, you'll find friends coming out of the woodwork everywhere to help, and of course, they've given me so much joy over the two years that I've been home.

Alistair Houston owned his farming estate, a shopping mall in miniature, the original venue for secret weddings and the hotel we had built, and he had stood by me all throughout the time in hospital. But now it was time to go back up to the hotel and start to take an active part in the running of the hotel and its performance.

I made a promise to Mr Salmi, who heads up the spinal unit of the hospital at Southport, that I would willingly go back to see patients who'd had an accident and were in a similar situation to me. One day when I was in hospital, a young man of about 26 came in to speak to us. He had come out of Stoke Mandeville with more or less the same problem with his spinal cord as mine, and had gone through the same pain as I had, thinking that your life has really come to an end and all you could do was sit around watching television like a bit of a zombie, doing nothing. He came to tell us the story of what had happened to him.

He was born in Kenya, and during the Mau Mau uprising, his father was battered to death while they escaped, eventually to arrive in England. He made his way in life by going to the College of Agriculture in Cirencester. But one day, an accident occurred: one of the tractor machines hit him and he ended up in Stoke Mandeville. Now he had a desire to go and see where his father was buried, so instead of doing nothing, he managed to persuade Land Rover to sponsor him with two Land Rovers which they were going to drive all the way overland on the journey from England to where his father was buried in Kenya. They ended up achieving this objective, and not only that, through sponsorship for his journey, they had raised sufficient money to build a small hospital near Nairobi for children who'd had spinal accidents.

He went to Durban to fly home, only to realise that the journey had taken more out of him than he realized. He had been suffering from bedsores from sitting in the Landrover for so long but had pushed himself and pretty much ignored them to get the trek done, so had to go back into hospital for about six months! But he came through it and was quite all right. He came up to Southport to talk to us and also went to Oswestry to try to cheer up and inspire the patients there.

After he left, I said, "By God, Mawdsley! If he can do that, what am I doing, faffing around?"

And today, I still think of him. He did give me strength and inspiration, amongst many other things, that have got me to where I am today.

So, slowly, in all aspects of my life, I began to break down the barriers one by one, and I'm now on the next one: my desire to write my book, the story of a hotelier, throughout my lifetime.

So, having broken down all these barriers, there you are. We'll see how we get on.

Life goes on whether you participate or not, but I have never been the sort of person who sits back and lets life happen. I have always lived my passion, created my own new projects and challenged myself to achieve in new areas. My mind and my heart are still active and engaged; my consultation work has continued, and I have continue to realise my ambitions—whether in the hotel business, hunting, or in photography and writing. Having mastered the use of a camera, I've just won my first prize for my portrait work.

Life is for living, and it's not over yet! I look forward to new challenges, and new solutions. Moreover, I invite you to fulfil your own dreams, to live with a sense of purpose, and to be of service.

John Mawdsley

Prime Minister John Major

The Three Mawdsley Children

John Mawdsley

Mr Khasbulatov Russian Prime Minister

Prime Minister Margaret Thatcher

Liverpool Fire Tender

My early team lead my Chef de cuisine

Gaby and I with Count and Countess Spencer in the Guildhall

The house we bought, later to become the hotel

The sales trip we took to Canada

The Countess Spencer

5876958R00118

Printed in Great Britain
by Amazon.co.uk, Ltd.,
Marston Gate.